From

THE
UNCUT JEWEL

A Divine Communication to Mankind

For darling
Rosemary
with all my
love + HIS
LOVE

THE UNCUT JEWEL

A Divine Communication to Mankind

———

Gerda Johst

Regency Press (London & New York) Ltd.
125 High Holborn, London WC1V 6QA

*"Your pure and sublime offering of divine words to mankind shall be
dedicated to those who are mature and strong in soul and rich in the
heart's power of love. In our world they will fulfil noble deeds for God
and will serve in the great work of creation in the cosmos."*

Benedicta
1st March, 1983.

Registered: Register of Copyrights, Copyright Office, Library of Congress,
                  Washington, D.C. 20559 USA.
Original Title: Das Ungeschliffene Juwel
First edition: (German) 1983
This edition: 1989
Translation by: Olga van Oppens

ISBN 0 7212 0779 0

Printed and bound in Great Britain by
Buckland Press Ltd., Dover, Kent.

Contents

Author's Foreword to the English Edition

EVERY translation of a philosophical, religious or poetic work can only be an interpretation. It is like a piece of music that has to be transposed to another key. If this can be done without mistakes, the optimum has been achieved.

The melodious beauty of the language of these messages and reports received from the spirit world places them in the category of poetry and I would advise every reader who understands German to enjoy them in the language in which they were given to me.

I would like the reader to know that I chose the title "The Uncut Jewel", because the texts are published exactly as I received them. Furthermore, although they have been assembled and are presented in chapter form, they were not given to me in the chronological order in which they now appear.

Over the years I received isolated messages and I have assembled and arranged them according to subject matter. It occurred that I received more than one message or report on a given subject, perhaps from a different point of view or in different words—as was the case with gods, angels and reincarnation—and I pass on these duplicate passages without tampering with them. The Gospels also record events more than once, seen from different viewpoints and reported in various ways and we would not like to dispense with any one account.

I think that every reader who is earnestly interested in this book will come across chapters or sections which he feels have been written only for him. And this feeling is correct, for these messages are directed to every one of us.

I have read this English translation with great pleasure. I hope that this gift from God, which I am to pass on to humanity, also enriches your life and brings you happiness and blessings.

Gerda Johst,
Rottach-Egern. 1988.

PART ONE

The Story of my Miracle

CHILDHOOD AND RELIGION

I WANT to tell you the story of my miracle. We call a miracle that which we cannot explain scientifically, or grasp with our intellect and categorise into the normal, the familiar or the ordinary. And yet, such a miracle is just as natural as life in its myriad forms. It is only that our rational minds have not yet managed to penetrate into the mysterious world beyond, the realm of the invisible, the flowing and breathing reality of spirit life.

There are people who know about it: they have profound knowledge or inquiring, investigative minds; they are devout or deeply religious. I was not such a person. I had a clear and healthy mind. I had received a good, all-round education. I lived, as you might say, a righteous life and I was content.

Until one day the miracle occurred. The world beyond broke into my every-day existence and I was confronted with the incredible recognition of God's reality.

Actually, the story of my miracle had begun in my childhood, but I had long since forgotten about it. A child finds everything miraculous: every flower, every animal. And heaven and earth are one. God, the loving Father, was as real to me as a human being. I took it for granted that I could understand him whenever he spoke to me. It never occurred to me that this might be something unusual.

My childhood was extremely happy. Although my parents were neither Catholic nor Protestant, they were not atheists and they brought me up to be religious.

We lived at the Tegernsee. The images of my childhood—the neighbouring farms and mountains, the glistening Weissach; the forests where gnomes and fairies led a secretive life among decaying tree trunks and roots; my mother's flower garden, the beloved lake; sunny summers and snowy winters—remain in my memory like fairy tales.

My father, who came from Hamburg, was a portrait painter. He had been raised in the Protestant faith but, dissatisfied with both the church and its clergy, he turned away from it, in order to follow his strong need for spiritual freedom.

My mother was a Baltic German from Riga. She had grown up in Russia, when it was still a deeply religious country. I am sure she was sometimes a little sad about my father's decision, but she conformed to his views, because he knew how to convince her. She often told me about the unbelievably beautiful Easter and Christmas festivals of her childhood, which we "unemotional Germans" could not begin to understand.

My parents met in Vyatka in 1914. Vyatka was the last Government town before the Ural mountains. They both spoke Russian. The Russian folk-songs were as familiar to me as those of Upper Bavaria, because there was always music and singing in our home. My father played the zither and the guitar and when I was six years old I had zither lessons. Later, when I was 12, my father granted my greatest wish when he bought me a piano.

I was an only child, but I was never lonely, as there were always children who came to play at our home and they were welcome guests. And the animals! They were all members of the family. The dachshund and the pomeranian, the tame raven, the canaries, the parakeets, rabbits and cats—whatever was brought to our house during the course of the years.

I was very young when my father drew my attention to the Indian phrase *tat twam asi: that is you.* We took for granted this Hindu-Buddhistic attitude towards animals; one which enjoins humility in the presence of creation and respect for life. In all the wonders of nature, in all its beauty and abundance, I was fully conscious of God's work.

Once I was especially impressed by a caterpillar's metamorphosis into a butterfly. I had found an unusually beautiful, long-haired caterpillar and kept it in a terrarium. One day it began to spin a cocoon. Starting at the end of its body, it laboriously wound thread upon thread around itself, until only the tiny head and shining black eyes were visible. Finally they too vanished.

I was sad to see the beautiful, beloved little animal disappear into its self-made coffin. I cannot remember how long I kept the grey chrysalis. I forgot about it. Fortunately however, my father noticed how it broke open one morning. He woke me and my mother and we watched excitedly as the butterfly emerged from the cocoon, tremblingly unfolded its beautiful wings and, newborn, flew off into the bright summer's day.

It was not until I went to school that I noticed we did not belong to a religious denomination. This did not bother me, as I joined the Roman Catholic and Protestant pupils alternatively for religious education. I followed our teachers' daily lessons with great interest and became deeply devout. Every evening I would pray to God and commit to him whatever was on my mind. When I had particularly important questions, I would even hear his answers—not with my ears, but in my head. This seemed quite normal to me, for my prayers too were not spoken, only thought.

I never lacked for comfort when I was worried or troubled. Childhood worries! I remember the day my dachshund ran away and I beseeched God to return my beloved playmate, I heard the reassuring words:

"Don't cry! Tomorrow the postman will come. He knows exactly where your little dog is and he will tell you, so that you will be able to bring him home." Promises like this always came true.

I never prayed to Jesus. The baby Jesus in his cradle, the Christ child who brings gifts to children on Christmas Eve and the crucified Messiah in his tortured suffering were concepts difficult for me to reconcile. I did not like to look at rural crucifixes. The portrayals of this cruel murder were too horrible. Nor did I understand the meaning of redemption that was supposed to be conveyed by this disgraceful death.

On the other hand, I had a very close relationship with the Virgin Mary. Portrayed as the queen of heaven in the large war memorial painting my father had depicted on the church at Egern (in the course of time this has been destroyed by the weather), she somewhat resembled my mother.

"The veneration of the Virgin Mary is the best aspect of Catholicism," I once heard my father say. And I did venerate her.

I was seven or eight years old when a religious education lesson plunged me into the greatest anguish. The lesson was about the meaning and necessity of baptism. I knew that I had not been baptised. Immediately after class I went to see the teacher, whom I was very fond of. She knew nothing about the omission of my parents. She looked at me in astonishment when I asked her how it would be when a person who had been baptised, but had led a bad life, decided to repent shortly before his death. Would he go to heaven?

"If his repentance is deep and honest, God in his mercy will surely forgive him and accept him in heaven."

"And what happens to another person when he dies if he has not been baptised, but has always led a good life—does he also go to heaven?"

"If he has not been baptised, he cannot go to heaven, because the holy ceremony of baptism is the pre-requisite for the doors of heaven to be opened for us."

I was deeply upset by this information. I cannot remember if it was for days or for weeks that the fear of dying unbaptised preyed on my mind.

I said nothing to my parents. Eventually I overcame my shyness and confided in the Protestant vicar, asking him to baptise me. The clergyman must have understood my distress. Soon afterwards he visited my father and, during the course of a long discussion, tried to convince him to have me baptised. I was in the next room, agitatedly following the argument of the two men.

"I'll baptise your little girl although you no longer belong to our Church. I'll baptise her, because I feel sorry for the child. She lives cut off from every Christian community, although she is a very devout little person," I heard the vicar say.

"This goes against my philosophy of life," my father replied. "You are asking too much of me."

After my father had explained his philosophy to the clergyman in very heated terms, he refused the request, saying that when I came of age I could handle the matter as I pleased but, for the time being, everything was all right the way it was.

That night, deeply unhappy about my inevitable final expulsion—as I saw it—I could not fall asleep. But once again I was freed from my anguish by the comforting words of our good Lord—words which I could hear quite clearly. Baptism was not as important as I had been told. And he, our Father in heaven, loved all his children equally, baptised or not. And then he promised me that he would definitely accept me into heaven when the time came, adding that, until then, many, many years would pass by, because I still had a long time to live on earth.

Very happy and relieved, I fell asleep after I had promised God, with a feeling of passionate gratitude, that I would definitely have myself baptised as soon as I grew up.

I did not keep this solemn promise.

ADOLESCENCE AND THE RENUNCIATION OF FAITH

IF I page further through my book of remembrances, I no longer find fairy-tale pictures. From year to year the sky above the mountains of my homeland seemed to grow ever darker. We were at war. And now the tie which had bound me to the Creator while I was a child began to break. It was not a sudden, total rupture, but a gradual unravelling, thread by thread and each separation left a painful wound which took a long time to heal. The heart's complaints and accusations grew so loud that there was no place for the quiet, familiar voice from the world beyond and the silence of the night was overlaid by the multitude of my own thoughts. Where was God supposed to be? Where was the heaven into which, as a little girl, I had longed so fervently to be accepted in days to come? Out there in space were billions of stars at distances so immense that the very thought was mind-boggling.

At senior school I belonged to those students who called themselves *gottgläubig* (believing in God). It was a fashionable term in Germany at that time for those without a particular denomination, as religious education had become a minor subject. I did not even want to belong to any Christian group, for I was gradually beginning to understand my father's philosophical views.

As a young girl I read a great deal. I was fascinated and excited by a book called *The Enigmas of the World* by the zoologist, Ernst Haeckel. In the chapter 'Knowledge and Faith' he condemns all religious belief as irrational superstition generated by false perceptions and fictitious images, in contradiction to the clearly perceived laws of nature. He writes:

"In Indian and Egyptian religions, in Greek and Roman mythology, in the Talmud as in the Koran, in the Old as well as the New Testament, the gods speak and act like human beings, and the revelations through which they disclose to us the secrets of life and try to solve the mysterious enigmas of the universe are figments of human imagination. The "truth" which believers read into them are human inventions, and the childlike belief in these absurd revelations is superstition."

Haeckel goes on to say that true revelation, which is true knowledge, is only to be found in nature. He also states that what we call "the soul" is simply a natural phenomenon, and the belief in the immortality of the soul is scientifically untenable.

But what kind of spiritual power has formed nature? What kind of will controls unconscious matter and produces all the miracles of life like, for example, the metamorphosis of the caterpillar into the butterfly? For this, the greatest of all the world's mysteries, Haeckel offered no scientific explanation.

Although the theories of the great zoologist were not able to convince me of the senselessness of our religion, I continually came across books containing descriptions of atrocities committed in the name of the cross—the Thirty Years War, the persecution of the Huguenots, the Crusades . . .

But the most terrible, and I assume the most decisive factor in my decision to turn away from faith were the crimes of the Inquisition, which were reported in the most horrific detail in these books.

During this period I often pondered over the concept of the devil. How was one to interpret this centuries-old image of the Satan of Christianity? An evil spirit who hated almighty God was conceivable only if one deleted the adjective "almighty". But that this devil should—contrary to all reason—punish in death those who in life had declared themselves for him and had succumbed to his suggestions (thereby harming his greatest enemy, the Lord God), I found completely absurd.

By punishing evil people he really acted in favour of a good power, whose purpose had to be to condemn what was evil. But the way in which they were punished! Eternal torture in the fires of hell was truly satanic and could not possibly be tolerated by a God of love, if he was almighty. Had not Jesus, who called himself the son of God, taught us these words:

"Love your enemies; bless those who curse you; do good to those who hate you."

I was deeply disappointed by the irresponsible indifference of the contemporary Church towards animals. Schopenhauer,* who claims justice for animals, whereas a weak, biblical proverb only requires

*Schopenhauer died in 1860. Today one reads newspaper headlines such as: *14 million animals used up in experiments every year.* Used up! What a declaration! And with such gruesome acts mankind presumes to advance.

compassion, speaks of the "shameful wickedness" with which our "Christian rabble" treats animals, without the intervention of the keepers of religion. He writes that Brahmins and Buddhists, whom one tries to convert to Christianity, are deeply disgusted by Europeans and their religion when they learn how animals are treated in Europe.

In Chapter XV entitled 'Parerga and Paralipomena' of his book *On Religion*, he fulminates against unnecessary vivisection and writes:

"Nowadays every stupid medical man considers himself entitled to practise cruelty to animals in his torture chamber in order to decide on problems whose solutions were published long ago in books, just because he is too lazy and ignorant to read them."

I once spoke to a young Catholic woman about this. She was only a little older than I and very happy in her belief. She said:

"A person who has understood Jesus and has accepted him into himself cannot possibly be cruel to either man or animal."

This was a beautiful concept. But who *had* understood Jesus? How many of those taking holy communion had really accepted Jesus into themselves, I wondered? For me Jesus represented a divine idea of love, a spark from heaven that had failed to ignite in the souls of men, so that darkness remained on our earth.

Haeckel writes that Frederick the Great, who was the first to prohibit torture: "summarises his conclusion in the following sentence: the study of history leads us to the conviction that from Constantine the Great to the time of the Reformation the whole world was mad."

And to me it seemed to be mad again. What an abundance of culture, art and the greatest intellectual gifts was possessed by each one of those nations, which we were forced to call enemies at this time. As a young girl I loved the music of Chopin, the Polish composer whom I discovered through my piano playing. My father and I shared the same enthusiasm for the works of French painters. I had a passionate bond with the English because of their poetry. And I asked my parents to translate into German the wonderful epics and ballads of the Russian, Lermontov.

There one was, young and filled with a world-embracing love for mankind—and everywhere there was death, destruction and extermination.

The years passed. And finally, when everything seemed to be over there was the most terrible occurrence, the result of the ultimate demoniacal will of destruction: the dropping of the first nuclear bomb.

Now mankind was overcome by the horror of the end of time and the feeling spread like a paralysing virus:

"We have no future anymore. We are lost."

Lost was the faith in a noble, divine destiny of mankind and for me, faith in God seemed to be lost for all time.

One evening during that sad, bleak post-war period I heard Schubert's *Unfinished Symphony* and I cried deep into the night for the Father in heaven I had once loved so dearly. He was no longer there. He had disintegrated in the remote distance of the universe, leaving behind his imperfect creation on this earth, doomed to destruction.

TURNING-POINT AND CHANGE

I will pass briefly over the next years of my life. My art lessons with my father and my piano lessons with a Munich professor were followed by years of work and a great deal of travelling.

After my marriage I lived at the Woerthsee in Upper Bavaria, where our daughter grew up. This idyllic period was followed—after we had been obliged to move to the southern outskirts of Munich—by three extremely hard years. My parents had moved in with us and both of them suffered strokes which left them severely debilitated. To care for them I had to summon up more strength than I actually possessed and eventually I suffered a physical collapse.

After the death of both my parents in 1976 I needed many months to recover. During my convalescence—a time of tranquillity and reflexion—I turned once again to music and painting and paged through old, almost forgotten books.

I was particularly captivated by the Bavarian author, the late Lena Christ, with whom I felt a close association. Her husband, Peter Benedix, who had discovered and furthered her literary talent, had been a close friend of my father and his second wife, a violinist, had been my very dear friend. In my youth I had spent many memorable hours with these two at their home in Irschenhausen in the Isar valley.

When my Uncle Peter, as I called him, talked about his first wife, he sometimes described unusual experiences that had occurred in her presence, because she had extra-sensory perception. Apparently, when she stretched out her hands and passed them before a glass standing in front of her on the table, it would begin to vibrate and circle without her touching it. Once some flowers suddenly appeared before her on the table, and she received many signs and instructions from the other world.

After her death she gave her husband unmistakable proof of her continued existence, until he asked her to stop for their childrens' sake. In his book *The Way of Lena Christ,* Benedix talks about these experiences. The book ends with the following sentence:

"However inconceivable and improbable it may appear that given the immense abundance with which nature squanders her wealth a shadow of our physical body should live on, one thing is certain—we are surrounded by secrets and unsolved mysteries, which should teach us modesty and humility towards the realm of the unknown which lies beyond all visible things."

Now, as I re-read the book after 30 years, I was overcome by a feeling, more than that, by a certainty, that I might also have extra-sensory abilities. One evening when I was alone—it was at the beginning of March in 1977—I tried in a superficial and inquisitive way to get in touch with the spirit world which, as Goethe maintained, is not closed to us. This experiment was so successful that it at first fascinated me, but later the mysterious communications worried me so intensely that I was unable to sleep for several nights. Like the sorcerer's apprentice I was no longer able to banish the invisible beings I had called up.

I do not want to pull aside the veil of oblivion that cloaks these days. Let me briefly relate an experience that was particularly meaningful for me, because it really convinced me of the existence of invisible entities with human intelligence.

Before it happened I had, of course, considered that there may have been natural explanations for my experiences and those of other people with extraordinary awareness. For instance, that highly concentrated electric currents in the human brain in co-ordination with as yet unexplored earth currents could create certain tensions that produced ghost-like apparitions.

It also seemed possible to me that some kind of secret radiation force in a person could cause objects like tables and glasses to move without being touched. An oscillating pendulum indicating letters of the alphabet could well have been the result of direction from the depth of the sub-conscious. To hear words and knocking signals could be a delusion, the result of mental over-stimulation and extreme nervous tension. But a dog's reaction cannot be explained by such interpretations.

When I first attempted to penetrate the secrets of nature, my dog had not been with me. Several evenings later one of these spirits whispered to me that it would be able to prove its existence with its "magic flute". I had only to go for a walk with my dog the next morning.

The next day I set off along a road which leads through an extensive area of farm-land. My dog, a cross between a German shepherd and a collie and a healthy, intelligent animal, was running ahead of me, sniffing along the roadside. Suddenly, loud and clear, a few steps in front of me to my right, I heard a broken triad—prime, third and fifth. It did not sound like a flute. The tone was somewhere between an aeolian harp and electronic music. The dog started and immediately leaped towards the sound. He barked, jumped left and right and in a circle and, with outstretched head, tried to sniff something. Then he gave another short bark and came to a full stop. He stood puzzled and gave me an enquiring look. When there was no further sound and after I had called out to calm him down, he resumed his inspection of the roadside and continued running ahead of me.

From this moment I was overcome by a feeling of dread. These spirits were real. And, as time went by, it became increasingly obvious that they had attached themselves to me with evil intentions, because they began to threaten me in the most terrifying manner.

I kept my experiences secret for several days, but then, completely exhausted by sleeplessness and overwhelming fear, I finally confided in my husband. I told him I was to die within a few hours. I was threatened and haunted by dark spirits and they had told me so. My husband was horrified. The doctor who was called could not calm me. When my anxiety was at its peak and a deathly cold began to surge through my body towards my heart, I suddenly and very clearly heard these words:

"White angels are standing at your side. Make the sign of the cross and pray to God!"

It was not until this moment that the thought crossed my mind that, if there were spirits, the highest and most glorious spirit of the universe—God—naturally had to exist. I had drifted so far away from faith that it had not occurred to me, even in my greatest anguish and despair, to pray.

But now in my mind I cried out to him, the Creator of life, and

But now in my mind I cried out to him, the Creator of life, and implored him to save me from death. Immediately I felt a warmth projecting on to me; it seemed as if a large, strong hand covered and protected me. Still in a state of extreme agitation, I begged a friend, a woman my husband had called and who had rushed to our house to look after me, to drive me at once to the church in the neighbouring village, so that I could be baptised immediately.

She conformed with my wishes, but the parson who was called from his home was dumbfounded and refused the baptism for which, he maintained, preparations were necessary. I was so afraid that I would die of a heart attack without having been baptised that I asked my friend, a devout Catholic, to administer an emergency baptism. She did so immediately with holy water. Afterwards the clergyman gave me what he called "the great blessing". He spoke good, Christian words and I calmed down somewhat.

The following night as I lay in bed, I was suddenly raised up to my knees. A strong force took hold of my hand and guided it up to my forehead, where my thumb firmly made the sign of the cross. While this happened I heard the words:

"I am Jesus. I have just baptised you."

The next day I was taken to a Munich hospital where, under deep sleep therapy, my nerves, heart and circulation were stabilised.

When I returned home, I made an effort to forget about all these inexplicable happenings and continue living as before. I managed to do so for several weeks. Then, one afternoon at the beginning of May, 1977 my whole life changed.

I was alone in the house and had been playing the piano for about an hour. I finished with the first movement *Andante con Variationi* of Beethoven's Sonata in A flat major op. 26, which moved me deeply. When I closed the grand piano and sat down to continue day-dreaming for a little while, I was overcome by a burning feeling of desire for God, whose help I believed I had felt so clearly a few weeks ago.

Suddenly I felt my right hand seized and it began to move. It drew signs and circles on my left arm, on which it had previously been resting. My forefinger traced my name, followed by an exclamation mark: "Gerda!"

In amazement I rested my hand on the table and in big letters the words were shaped: "God is above. He loves you."

"Who are you?" I asked. "Who is guiding my hand?"

My finger traced the answer: "An angel of God."

Quickly I fetched pencil and paper and surrendered my hand again to this strange touch, which enveloped it like strong air-pressure. In eager expectation and excitement I watched word after word being formed on the paper in an unfamiliar script.

The first sentence read: "You shall write a book about God and the miracles of the cosmos."

My thoughts that I was completely unable to do so, received the answer:

"You will learn everything. You will penetrate the deepest secrets."

"But will I be *allowed* to do this?" I thought. I received the answer: "It is your destiny!"

This is how I experienced the phenomenon of automatic writing for the first time. But it was not until much later that I heard this term and learned what it meant. At that time the event was, quite simply, miraculous.

Now I understood that my earlier experiences in March, which had terrified me so much, had only been a necessary beginning; a first step in the guidance back to faith by salvation from dire distress. On this occasion I was not afraid, but felt safe in the protection of this strong angel. And I awaited coming events with excitement.

THE ANGEL CLARISSA

FOR communicating with the angel, I used large format "conversation books," as I called them in memory of Beethoven. And, like him, I felt that I was hard of hearing because, listen as I might and strive as I might to understand the angel's words, I still needed writing to help me understand the faint communications.

As every ball-point pen or pencil has to overcome a certain resistance when writing on paper, I was advised by my angel to rest a little plastic pencil on a sheet of cellophane. This moved easily. Of course, the writing was invisible, but I could feel the letters as they formed and in this way my inner hearing was aided.

When I was able to understand my angel clearly in the upper area of my forehead, my hand remained still; but when parts of a sentence escaped me, words began to form. In this way I could understand ideas that were quite new to me. I called this kind of communication my "supernatural telephone". I still use it every day.

In the first conversation I learned that there are male and female angels. "I am a female angel. My name is Clarissa," my pen wrote. "God has sent me to you, so that you may be protected and educated, for you have much to learn. I will treat you both lovingly and strictly."

Not only did Clarissa develop me emotionally; she instructed me spiritually and exerted an incredibly powerful physical control over me. Whenever she seized hold of me, I was unable to resist. By her will she was able to force and hold me in gestures of humility and, until she let me go, I was unable to move.

Gestures of humility! Who in our time still knows them? The idea of kneeling down when praying at home would never have crossed my mind. On the contrary, such behaviour was so unfamiliar to me that I embarrassed myself, although there was nobody watching. However, Clarissa taught me to pray as the high laws of heaven demand. She forced me to my knees, made me lower my forehead and took my hands and folded them. She added wonderful words to my own thoughts, expressing a humble and awe-filled invocation to the eternal Lord and almighty Creator of all life. And I did not even know the Lord's Prayer!

The first prayer I received from Clarissa on 5th May, 1977 was as follows:

To God

You are God, the almighty, the Lord of the world. Your kingdom surrounds us, above us in infinity as below us in the universe of stars. Everything around us was created by your will. Be loved as the greatest of all miracles that we can never hope to understand. Not a breath of your greatness can be grasped by the mind of man. Lord, your power is unimaginable, and unimaginable your immense love for all mankind.

You are our weal and woe. There is no god besides you. We can never understand you, great, eternal God. Take, therefore, only the endless love of our hearts. Accept it and recognise it in mercy and benevolence. Your will be done. We think of you in humility, you, the greatest of all miracles. Your divine mercy is our hope, your love, our comfort. You are the glory of life, the power and the beauty of nature. Small and ignorant, I kneel before your greatness. My soul will always belong to you. Oh, you my God, I love you.

A second prayer was given to me on 27th May, 1977:

Take my Soul unto you . . .
In everything I see, my Lord, I recognise you. Your spirit in all
things lies before me. When I behold a flower, I sense your dream. In
every blade of grass that grows, in every bush and every tree I see
your work and sense your creativity. And over and over again, your
sense of beauty—everywhere.

In every animal I see, in all life around me I recognise your soul.
Even the stars, far away in the sky, are guided by you, my Lord. And
everywhere in nature, when my eyes revel in the glory of the world,
in the splendour of the sky, across the mountains, oceans, lakes, oh,
how I sense you my Lord! How full, how full of love and gratitude my
soul is.

You have given us everything that we enjoy here, and also placed in
our hearts the ability to experience all this, to feel the beauty that you
have given us in such abundant measure, that you have granted us so
gloriously and allowed it to come into being through your greatest
men, into whose minds you poured yourself.

How much you have bestowed on us through these men, whom we
love through their works. Through music, language, painting, through
tone and stone they have created by your will the works we call
divine.

There is great splendour in all things—in all love and all feeling,
that comes only from your soul. For it is only through you, my Lord,
that we humans love. It is only from your heart that we feel.

Take my soul unto you, take it in a mighty current unto you, my
Lord—and I fulfil my life.

Angels are able to fan us with a cool wind in order to demonstrate
their reality to us. At prayer in the early morning hours, or at night in
bed I often felt this fanning so strongly that I checked whether the
window was really closed. However, unlike a draught from an open
window that comes from only one direction, this comes from all sides.
It is particularly noticeable on the forehead and across the eyes.

I once asked Clarissa whether she created this draft with her wings.
She then told me that angels did not have wings, but were surrounded
by a radiation of light, which visionaries throughout the ages have
interpreted as a pair of wings. And it was with these "wings" of light

that she was fanning me.

In God's kingdom, however, angels, as well as humans were without wings. Subject to other laws, the laws of spheric gravity, they were able to move there as naturally as we do here.

Clarissa also told me that angels were bound by strict, holy laws. She explained to me that they can only be summoned by prayer and never by spiritualistic experiments. Table-tipping, knocking signals and similar manifestations were indications of low, earth-bound spirits.

I have to mention that in those summer weeks of 1977 my days were fully taken up by household chores and artistic activities. Portraits that I had begun had to be finished. On certain afternoons students came for lessons and, of course, my family also demanded my attention. There only remained the early morning or late night hours to listen to my angel.

Despite my happiness about her continuous presence, the thought that I was going to have to write a book was a heavy burden on my soul.

"You don't have to write—do what your heart commands," were the angel's words when I despaired after a first attempt.

Although I was ashamed afterwards and resigned myself to God's will, it still seemed totally impossible to complete this task. It also seemed pointless, because a book not only has to be written, it also has to be printed and presented to a circle of readers. I had no contacts in either publishing houses, or in the Church. And there was not a single person among all my friends and acquaintances with whom it seemed possible to discuss my miracle.

Being all alone with these mysteries was very, very difficult. At times I was afraid that the sentences forming before my eyes came from my subconscious after all. (The subconscious is one of the discoveries of our age that we probably take too seriously sometimes.)

Then I recalled the fact that on that day in March my dog had quite definitely not barked at my subconscious. In Clarissa's presence, on the other hand, he was quiet and content and when I felt her touch, he sometimes pressed himself against me to be stroked.

It was also absurd to consider that I could bring forth something from my inner self when there had been no input. Nothing comes from nothing, that much I knew. But here I was, receiving answers to questions concerning the cosmic world and reports on events that I had never heard about. And then there was this clearly noticeable breath of cool air, which was occasionally combined with a delicate, flowery scent.

But time and again doubts would assail me. Then I was afraid of being deceived because, after all, I could not see my angel. And how could I possibly be aware of the intrusion of evil spirits, which could confuse me and plunge me into disaster?

In these moments of despair I sent intense pleas to God, asking for powerful angel protection and for proof and signs of his love and might. From these prayers I constantly drew new energy for the double life I led.

The time came when I thought I could attempt to let my husband into my secret. One morning I told him I had come to the conclusion that our agnosticism was wrong; that I was convinced of the existence of a personal God, because I knew there were angels; I had developed marked extra-sensory perceptions and an angel was able to speak to me by guiding my hand—a fact which I could easily prove.

My husband, quite obviously extremely worried about me, implored me never to deal with psychic matters again. After a heated discussion he asked me to promise to stop writing in such a way, but I refused. Deeply disappointed, I realised that there was no communication possible between us on this subject.

Two and a half years were to pass until my husband, forced by irrefutable proof and deeply shaken, found his way to faith.

At that moment though, when I was alone again after our inconclusive conversation, I felt that the burden of my spiritual experience was about to overwhelm me. For a second time I asked God to take back all these wonders: the secretive communications with my angel and the commission to write a book and I received an answer to this prayer. First Clarissa wrote:

"God speaks to you," and then I received sentences written in large, broad letters, as though guided by God's hand; sentences of such greatness and sublimity of expression, in such powerful language, glowing with fatherly love, giving comfort and hope that I, deeply moved, was unable to think anything other than:

"I am yours, now and in all eternity. Your will be done . . . your will be done . . ."

After these holy and serious words of God and during the three following days, I received a loving present from heaven: in a profusion of questions and answers, some of which I heard clearly, others which I wrote down. I became acquainted with "divine cheerfulness". It was so enchantingly kind and affable, so happy and joyful, that it reminded me of the music of Mozart. All my worries vanished and I was filled with enthusiasm and exuberance, the enjoyment of life and the certainty of victory.

During the ensuing summer weeks my health also improved greatly. The traces of exhaustion and over-exertion that had dominated the past years of my life disappeared and I recovered completely. Now my husband no longer had to worry about me. And I never mentioned my miracle again.

THE COSMIC POWERS

WHENEVER possible I listened to the stories of my angel like a little child to a mother's fairy-tales. Everything I was told was fabulous and incredible and yet Clarissa emphasised over and over again that it was reality. She told me about the divine order of the cosmos and about the myriads of angels who maintain this order; about the sublime sons of God, whom she called "star-gods", whose task it was to administer individual planets, major constellations of stars or entire galaxies.

I learned that those sons of God who rule the planets close to earth are also called "angels of fate", because they have a strong influence on man's fate. The term "star-gods" is, in a way, a professional designation, serving to distinguish these important spirit beings from those angels of love and light who are totally imbued with the feeling of God. In contrast to these, the star-gods, although subject to the will of God, are free and independently acting powers.

"They are wonderful figures, magnificently dressed, just like kings and princes," Clarissa told me. "In build and appearance, as well as in character however, they are totally different from one another. Each one of them represents a different characteristic of God. They are all present at celestial festivities and the worship of God. They all meet regularly to discuss matters concerning mankind and problems of the earth. In the hierarchy of heaven they are personalities of high rank."

I listened to this account, but intuitively I was somewhat reluctant to accept it. I was so happy to have re-discovered the one great, glorious God, that the idea of so many under-gods seemed strange to me, although my imagination depicted them in the most splendid colours.

It also occurred to me that one of these sons might one day grow too powerful and act against the will of the father. Clarissa explained that this was completely out of the question. She continued:

"They are bound to God in a way that is difficult for humans to understand. His spirit is divided among them. They constantly feel the presence of his will; feel and fulfill it. A strong current flows to them from God. God dwells in their souls as he does in the souls of the angels and they kneel before the father in deep humility, just as the angels do when he calls them. Because they are eminent and powerful spirits who administer the stars, we call them gods.

"The word 'spirit' is inadequate for them and the word 'angel' does not do justice to their status and their activities, although they are angels. As cosmic powers they are not unknown to man. They have been called lords, powers, thrones, mighty forces, rulers, judges, sons of God or, simply, gods. They are also mentioned in the Psalms.

"Through telescopes man has gained enormous insight into the depths of the universe. Because of this, he has lost the feeling of security generated by the love of a 'father above the starry canopy', and is overcome by horror at the vastness of the cosmos. It is therefore necessary that you now learn about the universal inter-relations, in order to understand that this cosmos, despite its immeasurable vastness, is, nevertheless, ruled by one spirit—the spirit of God. This spirit flows out to all the galaxies, where it is received by the sons of God living there and is transmitted by them. Distributed in this way, it reaches every star of the universe."

In order to obtain information about the level of present-day astronomy, I bought a book called *The Universe Lives* (Walter Bargatzky, Econ Press) and read about the research results achieved with the latest radio telescopes. These results confirmed what my angel had told me. Let me quote just one paragraph from this book:

"Even in the Brockhaus Encyclopedia, published at the turn of the century, there is no word about the possibility of other galaxies apart from our own. In the meantime this optimism has been completely demolished. We know today that there are at least a hundred billion galaxies besides our own. In our immediate neighbourhood alone there are more than twenty, some of which were known to us but were considered for a long time to be minor nebulae. All these galaxies are separated from one another by huge distances. Even if we assume that each one of them does not contain more stars than our own Milky Way—which cannot be correct since there are huge supergalaxies—the total number of stars in the universe has reached the improbable figure of ten thousand million-million-million. And even this number will be out of date in a short time".

In view of these scientific facts, who can still believe that one single spirit rules over this ocean of galaxies, a spirit who, at the same time, is supposed to be a fatherly, loving God? What is the value of the individual when the earth is reduced to a grain of dust in the universe? "For God there are no distances," Clarissa explained to me. "He can travel to every star in the cosmos with the speed of thought, but he rules the universe from a spiritual centre with a power that you can only picture as a huge sun of the eternally shining Holy Spirit."

She advised me not to try and imagine the unimaginable, but to be confident in the knowledge of a truth not to be calculated in figures or understood in words. She finished these conversations by saying: "God is omniscient and omnipresent. A holy tie of love goes from his heart to every human being and he receives every ardent prayer."

She also advised me not to think too much about the sons of God who administer the galaxies of the universe as subordinate powers, for they were without consequence for us humans. It was God's will, however, that, at a given time, I would be given more information about a number of earth-related star-gods.

To conclude this chapter I would just like to mention that two years later I came across a book in which the star-gods are described in much the same way as I had been told. The book, *The Unknown Dimension* (Otto Reichl Press) is by Ania Teillard, a visionary of our time. The following sentence is taken from the chapter, *The Gods*: "The cosmic powers to which the planets and the lights of heaven, the moon and the sun belong have always been the same, even if their names have changed . . . we could call them gods, but we could also call them spirits, powers, beings in the cosmos who occupy an important office and are inexhaustible sources of energy for all men".

On the subject of angels Ania Teillard writes: "Angels are messengers from the world beyond. This is their true function and, in the actual sense of the word, their mission".

JESUS CHRIST

ONE morning in the middle of July 1977, for the first time Clarissa wrote in large letters the name: Jesus Christ. She was aware of my thoughts and knew that for me Jesus was no more than an historical personality, an eminently noble man and a prophet with very exceptional powers.

When Clarissa told me that he was Lord of all the star-gods, angels, seraphim, cherubim and archangels, I thought I had misunderstood her.

"How can a man who lived on earth only 2,000 years ago be master of the highest spirit powers in the cosmos; powers that have been at work for thousands of years, or have existed for all eternity?" I asked her.

She explained to me that Jesus was the most glorious son of the almighty Father, and as God within God—imbued with the Holy Spirit—represented the highest power in the universe.

"The personality of Jesus is of unique majesty and grandeur, and his love is infinitely important for mankind," she wrote to me. "Jesus is the great power of love through which mankind is led from the shadows of earthly life into the light of eternal bliss."

Only now I began to understand the deep truth of the Christian religion.

After the revelation of the angel, which shocked me, I went to the bookcase for a volume of poetry which, as I recalled, contained a poem about Jesus that had deeply moved me in my youth.

Entitled "The lonely Christ", I found it in an edition of Christian Morgenstern's works. Bewildered by the reality of what I had considered a mere legend and profoundly affected by the tragedy and immense magnitude of the destiny of this man, about whose life only scant traces and isolated images had remained in my mind, I read the poem again and, as I did so, an infinite love for this son of God who had become man flared up in my heart. And in tears of mingled pain and bliss I understood the terrible truth of the closing words: "And you sleep!"

The Lonely Christ

Stay awake and pray with me!
My soul is sad unto death.
Stay awake and pray with me!
Your eyes are full of sleep—
Can you not stay awake?

I go to give you
My utmost and you sleep . . .
Alone I stand among sleepers.
Alone I complete
The work of my hardest hour.

Stay awake and pray with me!
Can you not stay awake?
You are all in me,
But in whom am I?

What do you know of my love,
What do you know of
The pain of my soul!

Oh, lonely!
Lonely!

I die for you—
And you sleep!
You sleep!

The second book I picked up that day was an old Lutheran Bible I had inherited. Forgetting about all my daily chores, I started reading the Gospels. The following days I occupied myself with other books on the great religions of the world—books in which I found reports about Jesus and I received additional explanations on the subject from my angel.

Time and again the Russian words I had heard as a child and which I thought I had long forgotten, came back to me; my parents used them to remind themselves of their youth when they greeted each other on Easter Sunday.

In English they are: "Christ is risen!" And the answer: "He is truly risen!" This Easter greeting must have travelled across the wide plains of Russia like a huge wave of jubilation for many centuries before the faith was suppressed there. And now, in this singular manner I discovered that this old faith was the truth. Whenever I thought of it, tears filled my eyes: "Christ is risen! He is truly risen!"

An important element in the symphony of this dream-like summer of

1977 was a performance of Richard Strauss's opera *Salome* which I saw at the Salzburg Festival. For me two millenia merged into an hour and everything was transposed into the present. I was deeply touched by the song of Jokanaan:

"Behold the day is at hand, the day of the Lord, and I hear upon the mountains the feet of him, who shall be the saviour of the world."

And in another passage, in wonderful musical glorification, the words:

"There is but one who can save thee. Go, seek him, seek him! He is in a boat on the Sea of Galilee and talks to his disciples. Kneel down on the shore of the sea and call unto him by his name. When he cometh to thee and to all who call on him he cometh, then bow thyself at his feet and ask of him the remission of thy sins."

"And to all who call on him, he cometh . . ." I believe that after this festival evening all my feeling, longing and loving was one single call to Jesus. And yet I was deeply startled when he appeared to me two days later.

I was not praying, but just walking up the first steps of the house from the garden when my right hand was struck by an electric shock that ran up my arm and penetrated my heart. I looked around and saw . . . felt . . . knew: Jesus! One cannot describe such an experience. The only words that come to me when I try are: glory, beauty, love, bliss and humility.

In the instant of recognition the image disappeared. My view lost itself in the wide expanse of the fields and the distance of the forest, when I heard the words—as clear and as real as the whisper of a person standing right before me—with which now also he, Jesus Christ, called upon me to write a book that was to be inspired in the first instance by reports from sublime spirits of heaven, and later also by Jesus himself. And I received the blessing of the glorious son of God. I was completely unable to understand how something so wonderful could happen to me. My joy was overwhelming.

On a later occasion I asked Jesus to repeat the words he had spoken to me that day (it was 28th July, 1977) by guiding my hand. These were his words:

"I am Jesus Christ.

"Oh, my child, I have come to tell you that you are blessed. An exceptional fate is in store for you. You are pale and trembling. No, do not be afraid. A miracle has occurred to you; a great, holy miracle. Because of a particular radiation of your soul, we are able to guide your hand. It is the wish of God to inform mankind about his works. Many things that man does not know, he shall come to know now. Mankind is passing through a severe crisis and shall be saved. You have a great task to fulfill on this earth. As you have already heard from your angel, you are to write a book. This book will be a revelation of the miracles of the cosmos. Your hand will be guided by the most sublime spirits of heaven and also I will have many things to tell you.

"You, my child, are very fortunate in that you have been chosen to be a mediator between heaven and earth. Show that you are worthy of this task and resign yourself humbly to the will of the Creator. Continue to lead a normal life, but in your free hours receive our reports. Collect them and do not worry about anything else. God protects you.

"This is what I wanted to tell you. I bless you."

OUR LORD . . .

I CAN tell only little about what I experienced during the nights and early morning hours of the following summer weeks, what I was told and what I felt. The time had not yet come when I was allowed to write down the reports I received. In retrospect, I believe that God probably ploughs every human soul to its foundations and sieves it before he starts to sow.

Together with the depictions and accounts of the other world, at this stage I was told about my tasks and duties later in life and in the world beyond. And over and again I had to answer questions which were put to me as though I was in an examination.

On one occasion I faltered and thought despondently:

"I can't do all this, it's beyond me; God has chosen the wrong person."

Then I experienced for the first time Jesus, whose presence I suddenly felt, speaking strictly to me. I heard the words in vibrations that resembled the human voice:

"You can do what we expect of you. God asks no more of a human soul than it is able to give. Understand this!"

Taken aback by the unusually sharp tone of this reprimand, I now sensed the full implication of the word "Lord" when addressing Jesus. I also felt the happiness of the humility of the human heart in the recognition of his majesty when I asked: "Forgive me Lord."

How many people today are aware of the strengthening effect of prayer and know of the mystical power of radiation in the context of the concepts: man-God, humility-sublimity, request-reply, sorrow-comfort, fear-reassurance, weakness-invigoration, trouble-salvation, suffering-redemption?

And yet each one of us has been given the ability to think and thoughts are the language of the soul. How else could one interpret these supersensitive vibrations of the human mind? And everybody can send his concentrated thoughts up to the Godhead. Everybody can pray.

Whoever neglects this ability will, in the course of time, have one layer of dust after another cover up the "aerial" which we all possess. As we are used to thinking in technical terms, we can also compare it to a telephone that never fails. And it is with this small, incredibly strong mental control centre within our brain that we can receive and transmit.

What a wonderful arrangement this is, and how foolish we are to let it atrophy. To be able to pray! Always to be given a hearing, never to be rejected, never misunderstood, and always to know:

"I am loved. My mistakes are forgiven if I recognise them and repent." Even severe guilt can find divine forgiveness through the power of prayer, self-knowledge, repentance and expiation and through the deep and sincere devotion to the highest power of love and life.

And then this name that one only has to think of intensely in order to be fortified immediately; the name that envelops us human beings like a bell-jar of radiation, like a protecting cover through which no disturbance and no threat is able to penetrate; this holy, beloved name: Jesus Christ!

He who knows Jesus and loves him will never again experience misfortune and will even bear the burden that has been laid on his shoulders like a blessing, because he knows he does not have to bear it alone. Somebody is there to help him; somebody compassionate, sympathetic and wonderfully comforting; somebody who was human, although he was God, the son of God.

All the suffering of the world goes into God and Jesus is in God. These thoughts remind me of an experience I had one midsummer night in 1977. It was shortly before dawn when I was awoken from a deep sleep by several slightly painful electric shocks in my right arm. I knew at once: Jesus is here.

"Yes, my child, Jesus is talking to you," Clarissa said, and then I heard his words:

"Come and kneel by the window, look up to the starry sky and pray for God with me."

"I must pray for God?" I asked.

"Yes, for God to the Holy Spirit, a prayer to relieve his pain."

"God suffers pain?" I asked in dismay. "Pain?"

"Terrible pain. The torments of life are etched into his face. Only the Holy Spirit can soothe, can extinguish these pains of God. Pray with me, so that a human heart on this earth joins in my prayer."

Clarissa had already told me about the Holy Spirit. She also called him the Cosmic Spirit. So that night I already knew about him and understood him to be an all-pervading power, as well as a personality. But what a concept, what an idea that love and prayer from the holiest heart of eternity—the heart of Jesus—has to flow into this highest spirit of the worlds so that God, the quintessence of love, can be released from the pains he suffers through being bound to all his creatures.

God, whom we so often hold responsible for all the misery on this earth, needs this power to be freed from the suffering of life—the very life that has come into being through him, the spirit of creation. Only the Holy Spirit can soothe, can extinguish these pains of God, which will probably keep returning until all material life has been transformed into spirit existence in the spheres of light.

I was not able to understand all the words of the prayer; but I could sense in it the highest and holiest associations of inter-surging rays of love of the divine Trinity in the pattern of eternal cosmic laws.

Later my guardian angel, Benedicta, whom I did not yet know when this episode occurred, tried to explain it to me in the following words:

"God is the highest of all spirits. The happiness, but also the suffering of all life, enters into him. The Holy Spirit is the original power of God. Whenever Jesus, in self-absorption, prays to the Holy Spirit, it brings about a tensing of all cosmic radiations. The love of Jesus for the Father flows through the dark waves of pain and the impact of suffering and fresh currents of divine energy arise. But do not try to understand God and the concept of the Trinity as long as you still live on earth. In our world you will come to realise more and even that will only be a very small part of the endless wonders of the cosmos. But the great, divine secrets of the Godhead remain inviolable and forever beyond the grasp of the human mind."

In the universe there are stars where the angels of the Holy Spirit receive every ray of love, every feeling and every thought of every human being on this earth.

"The Holy Spirit knows everything that happens," Clarissa once told me. But we are human and such ideas are overwhelming.

So we hold fast to him whom we are able to visualise: Jesus. His image does not dissolve in the mist of incomprehensibility, but has clear, solid form, face and appearance. For he whom we can understand and who we feel can understand us, was once a human being, as real as we are and now is our Lord, man in God and the eternal power of divine love.

IN GOD'S FORMATIVE HANDS

SEVERAL times during these summer and autumn weeks of 1977 I experienced the sensation of being held by a force that was stronger than the power of Clarissa. Sometimes it was so strong that it took my breath away. It affected my whole body, but particularly my forehead, which was lowered and sometimes forced down to the ground, or moved backwards and pulled upwards. The feeling of pressure could be so strong that it hurt. But whenever I began to groan the pain disappeared at once, although the inescapable spell that bound me remained.

Before such seizures, which only occurred when I was alone, I heard the words:

"God is above," or "God is near you," or "I am God."

How does one imagine the immediate proximity of God? How does one explain it? Is it possible that the Lord of the universe personally bends down to a human being and embraces him? It is an incredible thought. Is it a radiation of his being in the form of an angel, a cherub perhaps, which touches us? Or is it a remote-controlled ray of his spirit, a physical effect of his will, sent to us from the cosmos? I do not know. But when such an experience occurs, the only feeling that one has with absolute certainty is that it is God.

We will never unveil, never penetrate the secret of God. And the ways in which he reveals himself will be as varied as the ways man takes to find him.

At this period of time I once had an experience I could hardly believe myself, because it was contrary to all the laws of nature.

It was a week-day morning. I was taking a short break from strenuous household chores and was lying on my bed, quietly relaxed and seeking mental union with God. Suddenly I felt seized by something akin to a strong air suction, and I was raised about 8-12in. (20-31cm) above the bed. I sank back, was raised up once more and heard the words:

"Feel the power of your God!"

At this moment my dog came bounding up the stairs, barking and threw himself so violently against the glass door of my room, that I thought the glass would break. Earlier I had locked the door because, like all big dogs he likes to open doors by pushing down handles. Paralysed with fright and unable to react at all, I was now lying on the bed again. The dog fell silent, as if ordered to do so by a strict command, and immediately I was uplifted again.

This counter to the law of gravity occurred several times more. The dog remained quietly in front of the door and I found him there later, resting without a trace of excitement.

Two years later and for the first time in my life I came across the word "levitation" in a book on parapsychology. The dictionary gave the following definition: Free suspension of the human body upon removal of the law of gravity. An ability ascribed to saints, yogis and mediums, for which there is no rational explanation.

I only experienced the phenomenon of levitation once; since that summer day it has not recurred. But time and again, over the years, I have experienced the touch of God, even if the intervals are now greater than they were then.

At the beginning of August 1977, when I was in just such a state of contact, I was asked if I was prepared to take a pledge of unconditional obedience to my angel—obedience during every hour of the day. I hesitated to answer.

On first reflection, always to obey seemed to me to be impossible, for how could I allocate my time, how could I meet the requirements of every-day life without my personal freedom? Once again I heard the familiar voice in a very soft but clear tone, almost like a physical sound:

"God is speaking to you my child, make the promise."

Then it became clear to me that an angel assigned to me by God would, of necessity, have to know far better than I and in advance what was to happen in my life and guided by divine wisdom, would never expose me to a situation that would over-tax or embarrass me in any way. I therefore gave God the requested promise.

From this moment on, Clarissa proved to be my mistress. For immediate communication, she gave me two signs. One for *yes* and one for *attention*.

Here I must add that I sense the touch of angels not only as a breath of cool air, or as heightened air pressure, which makes itself felt on my forehead, hands and body, but also very strongly on my eyes.

Clarissa's sign for *yes* was a slight double pressure on my eye-lids. Therefore, an involuntary double blink of my eye signified her consent. A multiple blink (much as our reaction when a dust particle irritates our eye) meant *attention*. This could be quite intense and then I knew that she wished to communicate something immediately and that I was to write it down. However, it also operated as a warning. Both signs were inconspicuous enough to be given to me while I was in the company of other people. I was not given a *no* sign. If the *yes* sign was withheld, then the answer was simply *no*. If still in doubt, I mentally asked the opposite question, which made it unmistakably clear what my angel meant.

The first order Clarissa gave me concerned a period of strict fasting, together with clear instructions for a healthy diet. Whenever I received the *attention* sign at table, I knew I had to stop eating immediately. After three weeks, when the scales showed that I was seven kilos below my normal weight, she ended the strict cure, saying:

"You have passed this test well; now you may eat as much as you like again."

Devout Christians have long known that fasting purifies both body and soul. I did not know this and it was not explained to me either. I just had to obey. I only experienced this once. In later years I was allowed to determine myself when to reduce the quantity of my food, and in general to live healthily and reasonably, as I had always been used to do.

The mental conversations with Clarissa delighted and interested me so much that I would have liked to continue them all day. But this was not possible. She was of such majesty and dignity that, time and again, I was forced down on my knees. When it so happened that I inadvertently began to talk to her in my thoughts, the way I would talk to a friend, she sometimes cautioned me very strictly:

"Don't speak to me in such a manner! Learn to control your thoughts and choose your words better! An angel of God stands before you. Understand this! I am out of God and God is within me. Therefore, always pay me the reverence and show me the humility that becomes God."

It is not easy to control one's thoughts. They come from feelings. Every vibration of the soul is immediately transformed into mental words. We cannot prevent this. We can only invalidate these thoughts by counter-thoughts, and we can apologise to our angel for wrong and unkind thoughts. If we do this, they are immediately extinguished.

Clarissa made me aware of the fact that words possess a strong, mysterious power; a power which can give rise to good as well as evil. People who dare to exploit this power for evil purposes, either through curses or through imprecations, are guilty of severe violations of God's laws and will be terribly punished by the star-rulers. The strong and positive word, however, is a source of happiness, for it attracts all the good and helpful powers. This is why the often repeated liturgic words are of great significance if they are consciously pronounced, like the prayer form:

"In the name of the Father, the Son and the Holy Spirit," or, from the Catholic prayers to Mary, the Rosary.

However, a thoughtless mumbling of these words offends the angels' feelings. Therefore, we must always strive, when we turn to God, to control unrestrained feelings and involuntary thoughts and to formulate clear, noble words that come from the depth of our hearts.

At this period of time my heart was full of love and urged me to pray, as if to make good, all at once, the decades of neglected prayer.

Memories came to mind, moments and hours of happiness. Like the first time I held my little daughter in my arms, saw her lovely little face with those big eyes and long eye-lashes, the tiny hands that closed around my fingers . . . and I without any prayer of gratitude. How full of joy I was during those years when our little one grew up healthy and cheerful, but I did not believe in God and never spared him a thought.

How could I have mistaken the miracle of life for a coincidental result of spiritless, unconfined matter? Can the building of a great cathedral be imagined without the master builder, who ingeniously assigns the workforce? Can undirected, random labour, even if it were to toil for millions of years, heaping up bricks, ever complete such an operation? Or the arbitrary, haphazard work of all those single, busy hands, without the guidance of a superior mind?

This is eternally impossible. Yet we, the people of this godless century, think that a child, this greatest miracle of life, can come into being without the spirit of the Creator.

When I looked back on my past, I also found lines in the book of my life that I would have liked to erase without the angel's knowledge. But Clarissa said:

"I know every hour of your life."

Once I tried to think secretly and pressed my forehead into the pillow, but Clarissa only said:

"I can always hear you."

I pressed my hands to my forehead to shield my thoughts. But it was no use. So I came to terms with the fact that one cannot hide anything from God and his angels.

But the angels do not only hear thoughts. They also notice every stirring of our emotions, see every feeling of our souls and even perceive those pictorial images of the mind which we do not express in words.

I have often felt the mysterious power of the spoken word. In particularly intense prayers a light shudder came over me and flowed through my body. It was like a cold shiver, but instead of passing over my body it passed through it. These shudders are acknowledgements of our prayers. They are cosmic radiations, Clarissa explained to me. They can be very soft and hardly noticeable, but can also become very strong and intense. They are always signs of divine love.

One night I felt an electric shock penetrate me like lightning and then spread evenly throughout my entire body. It was so violent that I thought one could die in this way. But I felt no fear, only wonderful safety in God's love and Clarissa's arms.

The day came when Clarissa said good-bye to me. She told me that she now had other tasks to fulfil and that, in future, my guardian angel, Benedicta, would take care of me. I was very sad to receive this news. The thought that I would lose Clarissa was terrible for me, but she comforted me and promised always to remain very closely attached to me.

"Every angel is a radiation of God—a vibration of his soul," she said, "and so your love for the angel enters him, makes him very happy and is guided on by him to the Father. We, the angels of light, are God's love in shape and person; we are the transmitters of his will. Even the most gentle vibration of his soul enters us and all our feelings are reflected to him. So, when you love your angel, whatever his name may be, you always love only God, and in God's love we shall remain united forever."

I never learned why God did not have Benedicta guide and educate me from the beginning, but chose Clarissa instead.

MY GUARDIAN ANGEL BENEDICTA AND OTHER PROMINENT ANGELS

A NEW chapter in the story of my miracle began with the introduction of Benedicta. To me she seemed softer than Clarissa, more gentle and more indulgent, but she told me:

"It is not that I am more indulgent, but that God *wants* me to be so. He wants to see you being guided more gently now. My gentleness can always turn into strictness, should his high will command it. You are held only by God, in the strictness as in the gentleness of his feeling."

When I asked Benedicta whether Clarissa was perhaps an archangel—something that seemed possible to me because of her strength—I received no answer. Instead she said:

"Archangels are keepers of sanctity and rulers of state. In the realm of light they have to master immensely important and difficult tasks, but they are no nearer to God than all the other angels. The hierarchy of angels is only a distribution of tasks, but we angels all have the same close relationship to God. Each one of us is as strong as God requires us to be at a given time, because we are permeated by his power and his will."

Now the time came when Jesus began to send the prominent spirits of heaven to me, to teach me the fundamentals of all those matters about which he himself wanted to give me information and messages later on.

Every instrument has to be tuned before a great master begins to play it. So, probably, I too had to be tuned before I could serve Jesus.

In the course of 1978 Benedicta mentioned many names and described a great variety of personalities—their appearances, their characters and their fields of activity; she also named the stars on which they live. Whenever I had a quiet hour, she had one or other of these spirits guide my hand. All the reports I received I transferred to the typewriter, because the writing was often very difficult to read.

Much of what the messengers of heaven told me, I found to be common Christian knowledge when later I studied the different catechisms, so I need not repeat it. Likewise, many aspects that I learned from the other world may already be known to those who have read metaphysical and esoteric books, or those who have studied Catholic mysticism. For me, everything was new.

The names of the heavenly beings were unusual and mysterious. Benedicta did not explain their meaning to me. To some of my questions she simply replies:

"Your angel is silent."

The first star-gods, as Clarissa had called them, that I came to know were Sixtus, from the constellation of Pisces and Usebius, from the fixed star, Sirius.

After getting to know Usebius I became acquainted with Ezenaidas, who administers the planet Neptune and later Abbenados, who told me to think of him when I looked up to Cassiopeia in the night sky. Osario, whom Benedicta compared with Baldur of the Teutons, once gave me an account of the ruler of the planet Jupiter, whom the angels call Emilius.

Ervinius, the ruler of Mars, also came to me once when I called upon him for help, which he granted me immediately and very noticeably. His guidance of my hand was particularly strong and firm. I was told many and wonderful things about Alemeila and Amerides, who beam their rays to us from Venus. I heard a little about Deiamos, who administers Mercury, but later he was described in detail in the messages from Jesus.

In poetic terms Benedicta described Samodian to me; he seemed to resemble the Grecian Eros. She told me quite clearly, however, as Clarissa had already done, that all these prominent spirits were not absolute rulers, but only sons of the almighty Father, who is our God and Creator.

She told me about Osseshua, the dark-skinned guardian and angel of fate of the black people. She said his appearance is glorious and noble. With fatherly love he seeks to help all dark-skinned people and give them the feeling of their own dignity.

For every human race there are powerful angels in the stars; personalities of the highest rank, whose appearance mirrors all the characteristics of the race in perfect beauty.

Sanaïdes, Endyminian, Alezebio, Mandenides, Melimeres are the names of angels who are only there for the people in the world beyond and, therefore, do not belong to the angels of fate. I was told that Domiegus is a very affectionate and serious angel of breathtaking beauty, who comes from the constellation Southern Cross to visit those who have to suffer a difficult death bringing them wonderful comfort.

I also came to know Dalamos, the son of God who comes from the most distant of the stars around our earth, because he came once and took my hand. He is the ruler of the Andromeda nebula, so he administers a whole galaxy. Despite the immense remoteness of his stars, he still maintains a close relationship with the earth, for distance is of no consequence for divine beings. Dalamos told me that the Andromeda nebula is the only galaxy included in the radiation fields of our Milky Way. All the more distant groups of stars are of no importance to the earth.

I read that the ancient Sumerians knew, as early as 3500 BC that the cosmos is saturated with life. They maintained very close religious relations with their star-gods. Now, once again, we are to learn that we are watched and examined by many eyes and not a few of us may be tried, weighed and found wanting. And when we have absorbed this scene of manifold activities above us, it is again sufficient if we simply turn to God, for all love flows to him.

Whenever we send prayers to Jesus, he sets in motion for us those powers which are necessary and appropriate to the matter. And yet we are also allowed, in cases of distress, to call upon those high spirits who are close to him and who are at work in the stars above us, just as we may ask strong human souls for help.

The Church knows of the power of pleas for intercession to saints, as well as the use of prayer by those among us who are mighty in love. If we feel weak and a strong soul prays for us, the love in our heart is absorbed by the radiation power of this soul and makes its way to the Godhead through a stronger current.

The intensity of the power of love is of the greatest importance. Currents of love, sent up to the Holy Trinity through our prayers, are absorbed and directed back to us. We do not have to reflect upon the manner in which God's blessing, the hearing and fulfilment of prayers and help is allotted to us.

If we should try to rationalise the divine registration and scrutiny of every individual soul, we can only imagine that the cosmic powers must have, at their disposal, techniques, compared with which our most brilliant computers are the most primitive instruments.

Devout Christians need no explanation for the mysterious activity above us. They have known about it for a long time. Did not Jesus say:

"But the very hairs of your head are all numbered," and ". . . for there is nothing covered that shall not be revealed; and hid that shall not be known." (Matthew 10/30 and 10/26.)

SIXTUS

SIXTUS was the first star-god whose acquaintance I made, probably because he comes from the constellation of Pisces, the sign under which I was born. But he is there for everyone. As the great physician of the spirit world, he is filled with intense love for mankind and is very often at work on earth.

He had known me from birth, he said, and had co-operated in every happy divine ordinance of my life. From him I learned that angels, like all spirits, have solid bodies, that they breathe and that their bodies are built according to the same divine law that shapes the human body. They do not consist of rays, as I had at first thought, but of matter of the utmost refinement, which is put together from "light-weight atoms".

Within our earthly body, firmly coalesced with it, there is a spirit body which contains each of our organs and each single cell. This body of very finest substance only separates from the earthly organism at the moment of death. It is what we generally call the soul, but it is also called the astral body. There is no earthly power that can damage, harm or destroy this body.

The breath of God flows through all of us. Gifted people can occasionally discern the radiation of the aura. This we see by the halos of Christian art. However, our eyes are designed only for earthly circumstances of life, which is why we cannot see our angels. But Sixtus told me that it is God's intention to refine the human eye to such a degree that, within a few centuries perhaps, when mankind has become more sophisticated, it will be able to see the angels.

Now this is only possible for a few people who are under the influence of divine grace. Such grace cannot be petitioned by prayer; it is always a surprise gift. It was granted to me by God only once, to have a visual impression of Jesus with my own eyes in order to free me from all doubt, so that I could quietly and steadily pursue the task demanded of me. To my question whether our soul which, in the world beyond, is a body, in turn contains yet another inner soul with feeling and sensitivity, Sixtus replied:

"Yes, you have another soul in your soul-body—a refined one with which you feel and sense. If this were not the case, you would be soulless spirits in eternal life."

On another occasion Sixtus told me: "Everything is vibration. Matter only *appears* solid to you. In reality it consists of very tiny particles, hanging loosely together. Therefore, I can put my hand through the table at which you are writing. But I cannot penetrate your body; it contains your soul body, so for me it is solid. When I take hold of your hand to write with it, it is not your earthly, physical hand that I am guiding, but the one within, which is of spirit substance."

Later he told me there was also the possibility of guiding my hand by power currents of divine will. At that time I believed I was the only person who had ever met with such a miracle.

I knew nothing about the experiences of mystics and mediums and nothing at all about the knowledge and insight into the world beyond, gained by para-psychological research. Only recently I read that even King David had received the building instructions for his temple plans, down to the tiniest detail of interior decoration, through so-called automatic writing. (1 Chron. 28/11.)

Sixtus is very often at work on earth. He has a large staff of helpers who are engaged in aiding mankind. And the saints, who are petitioned by people in times of sickness, are on the same level of vibration with him.

But the strongest power in this community of helpers is Mary. Sixtus indicated to me that his efficiency is increased when the Mother of God is addressed in prayer. In each individual case of sickness her love, her intercession and her commitment, increases his power and facilitates his work as a practising physician.

Later Jesus gave me a more detailed description of the personality and influence of Sixtus. (See chapter "Fighting Sickness with the Assistance of Spiritual Helpers—Sixtus".)

USEBIUS

BEFORE Usebius came to take my hand and talk to me, Benedicta told me that the fixed star, Sirius, is of great importance to mankind. Usebius reigns there as a powerful son of God and Jesus too is very often in the light spheres of this star, which is a meeting place for the most exalted spirits. Here congregations of our guardian angels take place and the angels of fate meet to discuss earthly matters and problems.

Benedicta described Usebius to me as being tall and slender, with a majestic appearance and fine features. Seen from afar, she said, he resembles Jesus. He is a great practitioner of the fine arts—of painting, sculpture and music—and takes care of those people on earth who, in harmony with God, are active in art.

Usebius came, took my hand and wrote much to me about God, about the unimaginable power with which he rules the entire universe, guides the stars in their courses, leads and governs myriads of angels and creates order everywhere, so that chaos cannot develop again.

"You humans must always look up at the starry sky with feelings of devotion and think of your Creator, whose exalted aim it is to populate the universe with life, for God is the spirit of life and love. There are already many stars on which life exists, but an infinite number must still be settled, for happy life must flourish all over the cosmos. This is why you humans are born on this little earth—to live on in the glorious realms of light, where you will be able to develop both mentally and spiritually. Always send prayers of thanks from your hearts to God, who called you into eternal being."

Usebius also warned me about keeping our earth clean—warnings that I am to pass on to mankind.

"Far too much poison is penetrating the oceans through your rivers," he wrote. "This leads to a disorder of nature, which will have terrible consequences for you. Also, far too much poison is entering the atmosphere. You know this, you know the consequences and yet you do nothing against it. It is very, very sad for God that in your greed for riches and luxury you have already exterminated countless animal species. Furthermore, the damage to the entire insect world through the application of poisons has serious consequences for you, because the divine order in the balance of nature is endangered. God grieves bitterly for every animal species that you exterminate. In a few decades you destroy what he has created over millions of years.

"All of us in the world of stars are watching your earth with the greatest concern. There is only one salvation for you: the return to faith and the strongest commitment of all mankind to Jesus."

Usebius also spoke of a necessary reduction in the birth-rate in the over-populated countries of the earth. However, this is not permitted through the "destruction of developing life", but rather through abstinence or contraception.

"The words of the Bible: 'Be fruitful and multiply and replenish the earth' no longer hold good for you, but rather, 'Preserve yourselves for God and preserve the earth for your descendants'."

We will receive thoughts, ideas, inspirations and inventions that are necessary to overcome all these problems if we turn back to God. Only then will it be possible for the good powers of the cosmos, which radiate over us, but especially for the individual, personal guardian angels to influence us and help us.

SANAÏDES

AN ANGEL who called himself Sanaïdes and who did not, as he told me, belong to the star powers, but to the group of angels around Jesus, once answered my question as to why one animal species must kill another in order to live and why there is so much pain and sorrow on this earth. He explained to me:

"God created life on earth from nothing. To preserve it, the severity of natural laws is necessary. There is no other way. Every creature is endowed with the breath of God, a power which maintains life and directs the organism. Everything inflicted on the creatures from their environment—for instance, when germs enter the body through wounds—is immediately countered by this life force.

"In order that the body's power of resistance can succeed there has to be pain, which forces the stricken animal, as well as the human being, to rest, so that the healing process can be effected. Therefore, pain and the fear of death are unavoidable and necessary for the maintenance of life. Animal species without the ability to feel pain would die out very quickly. These laws of nature cannot be circumvented.

"We angels cannot intervene out of compassion and take away pain from a suffering creature. We cannot, for instance, render unconscious an animal tortured by insensitive people, or hasten its release by an early death. However, angels can influence the emotion and the conscience of thoughtful people, and cause them to take steps against such cruelties and help maltreated animals. It is not possible for us to bring a healthy, strong heart to a standstill. A suffering creature is redeemed only when its entire system breaks down.

"We can also cause cruel and heartless people to be punished in accordance with a law of heaven. Their life on earth is then deflected from its predetermined path of fate and hardships, which were not in their stars, are introduced. Every cruelty, every brutality, every merciless act, whether committed against man or animal, is punished when the time comes, in accordance with the inexorable laws of justice. Men whose work it is to kill animals which feed people, have nothing to fear if they do this work as fast and as painlessly as possible. But it does occur that men in such positions become cold and heartless and so hardened in their souls that we must punish them.

"It is the same with scientists who serve mankind. Great medical researchers have tested their discoveries on animals. That was no crime, as long as they did not torture them. If, however, scientists lose all sense of awareness for the pain animals suffer; if they treat them like objects without feelings and souls, we angels know that these people are becoming "objects" without feelings and souls—they are forfeiting their humanity and losing the value of their souls.

"No power on earth and no worldy institution can force a man to act inhumanly. Take note that the atrocities committed in laboratories are outrageous! But they are not confined to laboratories. People abuse animals in the most disgusting way—cruelly, pitilessly.

"But if they themselves are in distress, they plead to God for evidence of his love, mercy and compassion. Such prayers will never reach God. Those who cannot prevent cruelty to animals by personal intervention—cruelty that is unworthy of a human being—should use all their spiritual influence to prevent it.

"We are hoping for an age of noble souls, a mankind aware of its responsibility towards creatures and nature. When doctors and scientists learn, once again, to listen to their inner voices, which are the angels' whispered words, when they establish a strong bond with God once again, it will be significantly easier for them to promote the welfare of mankind, rather than to indulge in experiments which, to a large extent, are pointless. Immense mental power lies idle, due to the fact that man has separated himself from God."

When I was on my own again with Benedicta after these comments from the angel Sanaïdes, I asked her why the Gospels did not contain any instructions as to how man should treat animals. She answered me that Jesus said and did much more than has been conveyed to us through the Gospels and referred me to the end of the Gospel according to John. There I found the following sentence:

"And there are also many other things which Jesus did, the which, if they should be written every one, I suppose that even the world itself could not contain the books that should be written."

EZENAIDAS

EZENAIDAS is the ruler of the planet Neptune. Benedicta described him to me as being slender, delicate and of medium height. His noble countenance is beautiful and soulful in expression, his character calm, dreamy and of the utmost sensitivity. One cannot, therefore, say that he resembles the Neptune of Greek antiquity, although water also seems to be his life element.

He once came to me in the autumn of 1977. The first words he spoke to me moved me very much and I will repeat them here because I have learned that everybody, without knowing it, is similarly loved by illustrious spirits from the moment of birth.

"Greetings to you, little earthling! I am much closer to you than you think. Because of your star sign, you are related to me by birth and I know everything that has happened in your life. The stars that shone on your birth sent the tenderest thoughts of my love and my soul's strongest prayers to God.

"My castle stands high upon a rocky coast. Its towers soar up into the azure sky, but its foundations are embedded in the depths of the ocean, which plays around the rocks. Never will you be able to grasp what immeasurable beauty lies hidden in this castle, in this shimmering blue palace of the deep.

"My world is the world of dreams and of beauty, of glittering melancholy and of wistfulness. My world is the water, it is the depth of the ocean in which lies life's eternal force and nature's elemental power. My kingdom is wave and spray, rock and shore, infinite expanse in grey-blue haze. It is the roar of the tempest in the dark of the night. It is the golden shimmer of the sun in the mirror of heaven. And like the image of my kingdom's nature, so is my soul."

Then, in thought, he guided me from hall to hall in his castle, whose miraculous beauty he described to me. It was the most splendid fairy-tale I had ever heard and yet it was only one shining page in the picture-book of my miracle.

Afterwards, when I wondered whether such a castle could be real, Benedicta told me that in the stars of the world beyond there were many such glorious buildings; and, she added, even on earth the great architectural masterpieces were created through divine inspiration.*

THE WORLD BEYOND—REINCARNATION OR ETERNAL BLISS?

TRANSCENDENTAL existence, the life beyond the borders of material perception is, according to all that the messengers of heaven told me, completely real; indeed, much more real than life on earth.

*Once again I would like to refer to the book, "The Unknown Dimension" by Ania Teillard, which I only read in 1979. She writes about Neptune thus: "He is the god of smoke and of dreams. The way he stood there on the seashore, lightly balanced against a rock and gazing into the distance with green-blue eyes, he was the very picture of sensitivity. His face was narrow, beardless and youthful, and sharply tapered to the chin. He is a seer and a poet, not a fighter. His palace is in the depth of the ocean, his kingdom is the most mysterious of all kingdoms. But never forget that the ocean, forests, localities and people we describe here are not made of earthly stuff. They exist in a sphere of immortality which seers have always known about, as forms of a transcendental existence beyond our own."

We all tend to imagine, provided that we believe in it in the first place, that life in the world beyond is strangely dream-like. In fact, it is quite different.

All the human senses are greatly refined in spirit existence. We have soul-eyes with immense visual power, with which we can see all the colours of that world more clearly, more beautifully, more luminously than the colours here on earth. We have the most accurate sense of hearing, the most refined sense of smell and taste and we are imbued with a feeling of bodily well-being such as we do not know on earth.

Benedicta once told me that we will remember our life on earth like a dark, cold and misty dream. For as we all remain in full possession of our personalities after earthly death, so we also retain our memories.

Only those experiences which we have to forget, impressions which may not be brought into the world of purity and bliss, are erased from consciousness. An angel gives us a Lethean drink, which causes certain memory images to dissolve, but it does not change our personalities.

Many people, among them good Christians, believe that after death they will be brought back to a new life on earth, which is to say, reincarnated. Reincarnation and the transmigration of souls is a topic which is discussed all over the world. The popular and growing opinion is that man has to improve the value of his soul from one life to the next, until it reaches a degree of maturity which will enable it to be accepted into the sublime spheres of the celestial world.

What I was told is that there are mysteries about reincarnation, rules, inherent laws, processes of achieving maturity and stability of the human soul substance in the course of the reincarnation process, but there is no endless series of reincarnations in the wheel of karmic entanglement. And yet we must not dismiss as superstition the experiences of other nations, experiences gathered over thousands of years in countries like India and Tibet, as some of our scientists and philosophers did with all religions around the turn of the century.

I am now experiencing for myself how clear and intelligible information from the world beyond can be and how realistic the contact with spirits. In these distant countries mediumistic abilities are by no means rare and there exists a great wealth of knowledge. Perhaps they do not know that even for them, Jesus has installed "dwelling places in his father's house", for the cosmos needs human souls, human intelligence and human power—that is to say, the energy from each one of us.

From all that the angels have told me, I have clearly understood this: Jesus has achieved that only those human souls who are too unstable and not sufficiently consistent to withstand the cosmic rays, have to be sent back to earth to be stabilised. The laws of nature are relentless. We all know that only the strong can survive. It is the same in the cosmos.

Therefore, those who fail here in their earthly lives—those who are not interested in achieving anything despite physical health and mental vigour, but only want to enjoy the pleasures of existence—have such weak and frail astral bodies that they would dissolve in the rays of the cosmos. It is the same with people who, although industrious and hard-working, active and successful, let their hearts atrophy and remain coldly egoistic and egocentric all their lives. Their inferior souls, incapable of love, could also not exist in the radiations of the Holy Spirit, which come from a sun of elemental power and permeate the entire universe.

"However, it is absolutely impossible that even one single soul should be extinguished. God would never permit this," Benedicta told me. "With immense labour, over an infinite period of time, he has created immortal souls and they must live on. God needs them."

The cosmos is constantly growing. It is expanding and new stellar worlds are developing. The universe must be permeated and guided by spiritual power. Therefore, man is a necessity in the divine plan of eternity. His biological structure was purposely developed as soon as the conditions on earth were favourable. The emergence of the various pre-historic animal species, which then disappeared, served the purpose of processing the life-pulsating matter, which had to be formed and conditioned in order to become capable of receiving the soul substance from the cosmos. Only after these preparations, which took millions of years, man, who had evolved from animal, received the immortal soul in the radiation of the Holy Spirit.

The love of God is in every individual soul and for this reason not a single one must perish. Only those souls unfit for life undergo a cleansing process and sink into a deep sleep. In this state of unconsciousness, the substance of their soul bodies is condensed. It does not dissolve, but contracts until the original form of all life is attained. So it is once again incarnated, in order to develop higher values.

This is how it was told and explained to me by the angels. It was as new to me as everything else I have learned. Later, in his magnificent language, I also received a message from Jesus on this subject. (See chapter "The Star of Preparation".)

In his series of messages, Jesus points out over and over again that we all live in the love, grace and mercy of God and that none of us who follows the way which he, the son of God, has prepared for us, must return to earth again. For the truth of the Gospel, which he proclaimed, stands above all other religious knowledge.

IN THE REALMS OF LIGHT

SO WE retain our personalities! And immediately after death we will awake to new life. Here is the first message I received from my angel on this subject:

"Every person who is incapable of committing an evil, mean, underhand or inhuman act and who has stood the test here on earth according to the will of God, is accepted into the kingdom of God. In the world beyond the most glorious life awaits the good, pure souls. Immediately after death, divine radiation is administered to every soul and it flows through the spirit body like blood. The heart begins to beat, the lungs expand; the newborn person breathes. An indescribable feeling of well-being flows through him. He opens his eyes and sees his angel. The angel leads him to a sphere where all those who died at the same time congregate. From there all the people are guided to their homeland in the world beyond. They are now free of all bodily imperfections as well as symptoms of old age.

"A big birthday celebration is prepared for everybody who enters God's world. He is received by all who loved him on earth, provided that they were noble enough to be accepted into the spheres of light.

"Nature there is of wonderful beauty. The people have again built villages and cities for themselves. They have created magnificent buildings and works of art.

"The constitution of matter is different to that on earth, but resembles it.

"All the incredibly large and splendid kingdoms are ruled by angels, who maintain order and justice."

Another angel wrote me:

"A wonderful life awaits you after earthly death; awaits all of you who have lived in a good and noble fashion. Always remember that on earth you only prepare yourselves for eternal life! Everything that you learn here you will be able to use in the world beyond. Nothing will be lost. Every ability that you have laboriously acquired through diligence and work, you will maintain for eternity. Your soul's hands assimilate the skill of your earthly hands and everybody takes all his knowledge and all his abilities into the realms of the spheres. Everybody is to be happy there. There is an infinite amount of land to be populated. The universe is constantly expanding, new suns and planets are being created and everywhere there are tasks to fulfil for you people who were born here, who grew up and matured on this ever so small but infinitely important earth."

ABOUT DYING

WE should all love our life on earth and endeavour to make it last as long and be as healthy as possible. Mentally we should always try and be ahead of death, which means integrating death into our lives. The daily protection we ask for in our morning prayers strengthens our guardian angels and has the effect that even the angels of fate—the star powers—are invigorated and influenced by divine radiation, to our benefit. This is what Sixtus told me.

Sickness and death are, therefore, not inflexibly pre-ordained. Everything inter-oscillates and even the greatest disaster can be rescinded by God's word and can be altered by the love of Jesus. As long as our bodies are able to fight against an illness, we should also fight mentally for our lives and the recovery of our health. If, however, it should be that the application of all earthly medical means, all natural powers and all the supporting currents of love from the spirit world are in vain, then we must surrender and prepare for the other life.

We often consider unjust what is in fact the most supreme justice, or a punishment of God what is inexorably woven into the laws of nature and biologically determined.

The most difficult death, Sixtus continued, is the one we consider the easiest—sudden, unexpected death. Through it, the soul of the deceased can suffer an emotional shock. But this only happens to people who live a life separated from God.

While still in full possession of their personalities, they suddenly stand next to themselves, next to their earthly bodies, which the angels call the vestments. They are aghast, because they confront a world they never imagined existed. Therefore, we should always bear in mind what lies beyond death and bind our guardian angels to us by thought and prayer.

Children who die suddenly are not terrified to such a degree. They accept miracles more readily than adults. Every child that dies is immediately taken into the protection of a motherly, loving angel when it awakens to new life. Everybody who has lived with close, inner ties to God awakens in the arms of his angel. But even unbelievers are received by spirit leaders and brought to a zone of education and maturation.

Whoever had a mis-spent life here is taken to a planet of purification. Hardened sinners and criminals are brought to the world of shadows. Alternatively they are banished to the earth. Here, at the place of their crime, they have, first of all, to suffer what they inflicted on other people. Brutality to animals has to be atoned for in a similar way.

The worst crime is the murder of a defenceless victim. The more intelligence a person possesses, the harder the punishment for his crime. Only those who are really guilty are charged with war crimes, especially those who provoked wars. (See chapter "The Spheres of Purification".)

People with mental disorders only find their own ego after their life on earth. For them the real life begins after the one they had to spend here in mental confusion or mental derangement. They are, of course, not held responsible for any of their actions.

The greatest mistake a person can make is to commit suicide, for the problem from which he sought to escape is by no means solved; he takes it to the world beyond as a heavy burden. Escape from life can be forgiven only under special circumstances—youthful immaturity; unusually terrible situations, such as occur in wars; great pain and mental confusion. In most cases, however, people who willfully terminated their lives because they surrendered to despair instead of turning to God in their distress, are sentenced by the archangels to spend the remaining years of the life that had been assigned to them in darkness, far from God—a truly sad destiny.

Those who have lost a relative or a loved one in this way can help him by prayer. This also holds good for anybody who has done wrong and has died. Often a few intense, heart-felt prayers to God or Jesus help to redeem an unfortunate soul. It is also a great help for those who have died if one attends holy communion and there asks Jesus for pardon and redemption for those laden with guilt. Every soul will eventually be redeemed and after atonement will be brought to a higher sphere, a sphere of light, where he can develop further.

If married couples or lovers are separated by death, and the remaining partner engages in a new commitment, there are no problems or conflicts of the heart when they meet again in the world beyond. Everybody is united with the one and only soul for him or her. These unions are not left to chance, but are arranged by angels who know the degrees of vibration and waves of sensitivity of every soul. Every union is the total and blissful fulfilment of the values of both souls.

All these things I learned from the angels in the course of the years 1977-1978, before I received the messages from Jesus. But now I want to give an account of how my life developed around these miraculous events which, at first, I had to keep secret.

FRIENDS

MY first confidante was one of my childhood friends from the Tegernsee valley. She understood the great importance of the divine injunction given to me and arranged an interview for me with the canon of the Munich arch-diocese. After he had listened to my story, he said:

"You are a mystic. Such talents are not unknown to the Church."

He mentioned some names, Hildegard of Bingen, Theresa of Avila and others, which were all unknown to me at that time. Afterwards he presented my first manuscript, which did not yet contain the great declarations of Jesus, to a circle of theologians, but they refused to concern themselves with transcendental perceptions.

Apart from the sympathy of my friend, I still faced this immense happening alone. And in this way I knew I was not going to be able to complete the mission God had given me—to write a book. I needed people in whom I could confide, and who would not only show understanding for my miracle but would welcome it with true and heart-felt enthusiasm. I needed help, advice and friendship. In the spring of 1979 I turned to the Holy Trinity with an intense prayer, asking for release from my spiritual isolation.

Suddenly events began to mesh and within a few weeks I met people who, each in their own way, became important and indispensable to me. Even my old friends, in whom I now confided, recognised the greatness of the revelations made to me and offered every possible help. They all witnessed the miracle of the direct transmission of the angelic messages through my automatic writing. The response to their most personal thoughts, sensations and experiences, about which I knew nothing and the loving messages from their own guardian angels who took my hand and communicated through me, deeply moved everybody who experienced it.

I was not only able to convey the words of the guardian angels to people close to me, but also Sixtus' help and advice.

Now, finally, I was no longer alone, but had sympathetic hearts in whom I could confide all the marvels I experienced, and to whom I could read every one of the newly received messages.

When, in November 1979, I invited all my friends together for the first time, Usebius suddenly took my hand and wrote the following words:

"Submit yourselves in my name to the service of the son of God. The holy light of truth will penetrate the darkness of ignorance. Be strong in your belief and do not allow yourselves to be discouraged. Behold, the earth is threatened. The great crowd of helpers—the host of angels—stands prepared to prevent the end of this human race, which has torn itself away from God's heart.

"Behold, the end of this human race can be seen. It can be seen from faraway stars, because the emptiness of hearts reveals itself a billion-fold. Only those who pray, who give themselves from the depth of their souls to the most exhalted of spirits, Jesus Christ, are destined to resist the downfall. You can read the downfall in the constellation of the stars, but all of you who recognise God are bound for a different destination.

"Send holy hope up to heaven! Seek to win individual hearts and kindle the strongest of feelings within them. God needs individuals! Hear the warning of the heavenly messenger. Never surrender to despair, even if the shimmer of hope seems to be extinguished! The strongest spirit powers stand over you, all of them bound to you by the magic cord of love. You must overcome the governors of destruction.

"The prevailing trends must be over-ruled by the enlightenment of the minority. Now pass on to others what you have learned, and rise

from the depths of sorrow to the eternal salvation of the heart. Bind
yourselves to those spirit powers of God that you know and whose
strength you will increase through the current of love.

"Let Jesus be visible to you every hour. Seek solitude for fervent
prayer and the salvation of earth as well as the grace of heaven will be
prepared for you. Oh, you do not know how strongly individual prayer
soars up to heaven!"

From this day on we called ourselves "The Usebius Circle".

After I had received the first part of Jesus' messages, we decided to
publish a limited edition of them. Because we thought that people
might doubt, or even consider it impossible that they could be personal
statements from Jesus, we thought to present them as messages from
angels. Whereupon, in very energetic writing, I received the following
instructions from Jesus:

"These events shall be communicated to mankind without any
changes. I am Jesus and my words need no interpretation. Strive to
present to chosen souls the treasure you have received as an uncut
jewel, for it is in its unpolished state that this divine gift shines most
brightly. Great souls comprehend greatness; inferior souls dismiss it.
Do not weaken the power of my personal declarations. It is indeed I,
Jesus Christ, who talks to you. Understand this and be happy."

In March 1980 we published the first of the messages entitled "I am
the Way—the Return to Faith" and presented this publication to a
larger circle of friends. In July 1981 we were able to add another small
volume.

In the summer of 1980 a father from Rome who had read my
writings came to visit me. He showed great interest in my miracle. In
the following years he visited me whenever he came to Munich.

After the second publication he pointed out that the appellation
"star-gods" for the divine sons who administer the stars might confuse
Christians. They could be called "star-spirits", "star-powers" or simply
"powers" but "gods" in the way it was understood in Greek antiquity
seemed inappropriate to him, for there was only one God; the God of
the Holy Trinity.

Since I did not dare to change anything in the messages, I turned to
Mary as the patroness of the Church, and asked her for advice. She
offered me the following words:

"Sometimes Jesus calls these powers "star-gods". It is a term of
brotherly love, for they stand above time in divine sovereignty. In the

language of heaven they are called "Theobrids". They are cosmic authorities of order and reflectors of the pulsations of the Holy Spirit, the Spirit of God.

"As you are a newcomer to this knowledge, seek to spread it without requesting the rejection of the term "star-gods" by substituting other names. It is a minor point and does not constitute a correction of what Jesus has told you. It is intended only as an indication, an explanation for people who think as Christians, for they must not be disturbed in their deep-rooted belief, which does not allow them to accept the term "gods". We wish to take the path of conciliation."

Here I wish to add that I received this message from Mary in my little "forest chapel". This is how I call a little clearing in the forest where a former field crucifix stands. In the summer of 1978 I found this beautifully made crucifix through providence. It stands in a spruce forest, quite hidden away and forgotten. Some birch trees are grouped around it. No paths lead to the clearing. The dilapidated little bench in front of the crucifix I have repaired for my own use. This idyllic spot has become a place of devotion and prayer for me. Here I can understand the words from the world beyond particularly clearly, just as in some churches and places of pilgrimage.

In August 1982 I received a detailed letter from the father in Rome, in which he wrote of his conviction that there was no reincarnation. Again I turned to Mary in my little forest chapel, this time with the reflection that possibly the Church might be reluctant to acknowledge, as the truth, what Jesus had communicated to me. From Mary I received no answer, but Jesus himself gave me the following explanation by guiding my hand:

"The Church is not reluctant to acknowledge the blessing of the divine revelations given to you. It does not refute the process of maturation of souls in the darkness of the educational zones. You have been chosen to transmit divine messages. You knew nothing of the principles of the Church. Now it is God's will that it be understood as you have received it.

"The servants of God should be happy about the fact that reincarnation is woven into the seam of eternity. So the spirit of God demonstrates that all life matures. A new point of view does not cause old values and truths to be desecrated.

"As every plant can only grow and flourish in ground which is suitable for it, so human souls only grow and flourish under particular conditions of life. This means that one single way of development would never suffice for all people on this earth.

"I gave mankind the expectation of eternal life in bliss, but I taught that only the commitment to me opens the way into this world. By no word did I declare that everybody—without a review of the value and quality of his soul—would find unconditional access into the kingdom of heaven. By no word did I decide that *all* men on this earth will be accepted into the kingdom of God before their souls have matured. I did not state that it was a sin to believe in the reincarnation of souls. The reincarnation of the souls of immature people belonged to those secrets which I did not unveil during my life on earth."

ABOUT THE MESSAGES

AS an uncut jewel—the texts given in this book have not been altered, I present to the public the messages of Jesus and the statements of Mary and the angels. In doing so I realise that I am merely an instrument; one instrument in a huge orchestra. But the divine symphony can only resound in the fullness and harmony of all the instruments.

All the words and messages we receive from God, all the images given to us in visions are probably only a breath of reality, a breath of eternal truth, which is as much as we are able to bear. In a new Catholic catechism I read:

"In his biblical revelation God adapted himself to the power of comprehension of men; he talked to them in a manner they could understand through deeds and events, through insights that he allowed them to gain and by words which he had them make known. When men testify that God has spoken, the least we can do is listen."*

I testify that Jesus Christ has spoken to me in a manner suited to my mental capacity and that he has given me insights and words that I must make public.

What I have learned does not contradict the old doctrines of Christianity, but amplifies the knowledge we have to date. And new revelations are being given to us. If we do not seek firm ties with God

Message of Faith commissioned by the Bishops of Augsburg and Essen. Edited by Andreas Baur and Wilhelm Plöger. 1979.

now, we will go under. Every person must understand that he plays an important role here, which infinitely extends beyond life on earth.

Jesus is now calling hosts of angels into action to save us from destruction and to lead mankind to a happy new age of maturity and great spiritual culture. Let us be receptive to these celestial spirits, who can only guide us if we open our hearts and souls.

May the following words of joy, which I received from Jesus at Easter 1982, fill our hearts and introduce the messages.

TELL EVERYONE

"TELL everyone you love: happiness is near for Jesus is happy! Do you see the silver strip on the horizon? With the dawning of a new age it expands. Be happy for the future, for powerful rays are being guided to the earth from cosmic suns.

"Oh, you people, you have committed evil deeds! Oh, you faithful, this earth needs light! Oh, you who pray, it is time you were victorious!

"Gather around me! Cast aside the burden of life and grasp its glory.

"The spirits of destruction are powerless if you join the son of God; they are insanity, avarice, hate and envy. They have raged for thousands of years; they have brought blood and tears, pain and misery to mankind. They have invaded the halls of the inner sanctum and desecrated the name of the Church.

"Christians of all nations have decried and scorned the commandment of love, the commandment of mercy, the commandment of respect to the Lord and his creation, the commandment of the holy transubstantiation, which should take place in all of you, as it does in bread and wine.

"Do not dig for the coffins in which my most sacred expectations crumbled to dust and ashes. Sentence has been pronounced on all those who allowed the heritage of evil to rise in their blood. Do not dig for their bones, do not seek the number and the extent of their terrible deeds. Mankind is weak and burdened and yet it contains the seed of the divine.

"Be happy now, for the change is beginning. As you are certain of God's grace even in this world, in the world beyond you shall participate in the light, which God's love radiates across the entire universe. You shall develop further on flourishing stars. May the hardships and suffering of life on earth only remind you of my life.

"I shall forget the pain of God I suffered for your sake if the most sacred love flows to me from a multitude of hearts! Through the power of this love I maintain the earth and now direct the first rays of a new age on to you.

"Be certain of this: the page of history is being turned and a pure white new page is being opened before God's eyes.

"Hallowed are those who awake early, for theirs is the divine morning which sprinkles them with dew in heavenly consecration. Oh, my people, be blessed, you whose eyes sparkle and whose hearts shine! Be blessed in God's infinite love!"

Jesus Christ

PART TWO

Messages from Jesus

ON THE TRANSMISSION OF DIVINE STATEMENTS

"AT THE end of this 2,000 year era which leads to a new age, mankind will receive very many messages from God, from the angels of God and from the most illustrious spirits of heaven. These messages will be transmitted by particularly gifted recipients, but there will also be communications through thought influence, enlightenment and profound knowledge and an understanding of God's holy plan.

"Draw your conclusions from the sum total of what is given to divinely inspired people. If the contents of the various statements do not always seem to coincide, bear in mind that all those who transmit the love of God are only instruments. Every one has its specific character and its specific basic tuning. An absolutely pure, divine statement could only be made by an angel. But you cannot hear his voice. Therefore, accept what chosen people communicate to you."

THE ESSENTIAL LIKENESS

"MY people, you who doubt the reality of God as revealed in Jesus Christ, hear my words: I am God! I am God's soul, I am God's feeling, I am God's will and God's word.

"I lived as a man, and as a man I loved and beheld the stars of eternity. As a man I suffered bodily pain, the anguish of humiliation and the fears of the dangers that threatened me. As a man I exhausted life's content to the utmost.

"As God I was born to the chosen, blessed lady, whose soul shone in greatest purity.

"She gave birth to the son who was begot by the powerful love of the most sublime spirit, by the powerful love of God, who in manly essence expressed himself in the preparation of earthly life and implanted the great miracle of the divine origin of the soul into human nature.

"This is what humanity believed for generations, ever since the spreading of the Gospels. But modern mankind deems itself wiser, deems itself more enlightened and refuses to accept the divine nature of him, who was born as man. Raise yourselves now from the shadows of ignorance to the heights of the light of divine truth:

"Jesus Christ is the son of God, he is the voice of God which you must heed.

"Jesus Christ works in the will of the Creator, in his feeling, in his blessing. He is God's power of love, in tune with the triad of divine harmony.

"Even as the third complements and determines the musical triad, Jesus works in the spheric accord of the divine trinity, in the trinal star of the Godhead.

"The spheric accord resounds only as unity – unity is divine power."

APPEAL

"MY aim is to save mankind from destruction. To achieve this, I need the collaboration of all noble souls. A mighty current of faith must flow across the entire earth and rise up to God's eternal world of stars.

"Behold, you are all the Father's children. Nobody is alone, nobody must believe that he is lonely. You are all bound to God by rays of love. The pain and suffering on earth will pass, but the vital power of the Holy Spirit within you will remain forever. Accept these statements as the truth. Understand that God's human son wants to guide all his lost and errant siblings back to the Father.

"I search for you, I call you, I love you! My arms are wide open, come to my heart!

"Be assured, the morning sun sends forth its first rays. A new day dawns in the history of mankind.

"Mighty is the power of the mind. The words of those who pray are weapons against all that is evil and rotten on this earth. Rejoice my people! And unite in this joy.

"Tell everyone: Jesus has come! He sends light into your hearts and happiness into your lives on earth.

"Now the stars are turning, and no one must fear for the future any longer. Now I give my life to you for the second time.

"But not as earth-born man, as God I give you all the power of love I possess. I want to work among you day and night.

"A host of powerful angels is in my service. A wave of love will overflow the borders of countries. In the age to come, wars will belong to the historical past. On all questions at issue, the nations will come to peaceful agreements. The educated and knowledgeable people of all nations must work with all their might for the purity and order of the earth, against the interests of those who do not want to listen to reason. It is absolutely necessary that the politicians take the warnings of the scientists seriously and consider them more important than anything else.

"I shall achieve my goal, but I expect your co-operation. Use every mental power for the good deed. Bind your souls to God and give all the love of your hearts to the son of the Creator."

THE ORGANISATION OF GOD'S STATE

"GOD'S state is organised in accordance with the most sacred laws. It is governed by divine justice. Imagine God as the ruler of an infinitely large kingdom; the son who is telling you this, is at his side; behind them, shining like a sun, the Holy Spirit.

"Next to God are ranged the archangels, the highest and most sublime statesmen. Some of them are familiar to you, but there are many others who have great tasks to fulfil in the universe. Subordinate to them is the host of star-gods, the rulers of the stars. They too are angels. They are divided into those who work in the cosmos and those who are earth-related. The latter are also called angels of fate. Every cosmic star ruler commands a galaxy, and there are billions.

"The angels of fate have other tasks. They are appointed to educate mankind and exert their influence on you from the stars surrounding the earth, according to the laws of a justice which is beyond your understanding.

"A strong current links all the authorised spirits of heaven to God the Lord, whose will commands the whole universe.

"Next to the star rulers, who are very independent, there are, on the same footing, the hosts of angels, who have a relationship of total unity with God. His feeling is their feeling. In the world beyond, as well as on earth, they work in the most diverse fields. Here, they are guardian angels. They strengthen you and inspire you. They take care of you and protect you from evil influences. But they have no power over fate.

"Mary, the queen of heaven, is glorious in God's light. She has great power. A whole realm of stars belongs to her and from here she exerts her influence in favour of those who pray to her.

"All the saints are in her service; they are authorised to help those who pray and whose hearts are pure. But even Mary, with all the souls who flock around her, is not empowered to intervene in every destiny. She too is subject to the sublime laws of the eternal rulers of fate. However, if the basic requirements are met, Mary, in her infinite love and mercy, can help the supplicants.

"Star rulers can alter a pre-arranged fate. They are the builders of your earthly existence and constantly watch you. If you pass the tests of these angels of fate, they cancel radiations of hardship and substitute more auspicious ones.

"It is time now for you to get to know them, for in the centuries to come you must pass through this short, but infinitely important earthly existence in respectful communion with these mighty representatives of God."

THREE SUNS IN THE UNIVERSE

"HOLY waves of light flood the cosmos. They arise from the constellation of unity of the trinal Godhead. This constellation consists of three suns, every one of which is of vital importance to the universe.

"When I, Jesus Christ, had demonstrated the power of love by sacrificing myself as a human being and ascended from human life, the third of these suns came into being. Through the immense increase of light generated in the world of spheres, the powers of darkness were forced to flee the cosmos.

"Through this illumination of the entire cosmos, God achieved absolute rule over the kingdom of eternity, which he had steered through the storms of chaos to the order of evolution. And at this period of time, God installed a star ruler in every galaxy to consolidate his might.

"Like all angels of the Eternal One, these princely sovereigns of the star masses are permeated with the spirit and the will of God. As they have sprung from the soul of the Holy Spirit, their feeling is at one with the Godhead, to whom they belong for eternity. Because of this and according to the divine laws of life, it has become quite impossible for spirits of resistance ever to develop again in the cosmos.

"The cosmos emerged from the darkness into the light when I, Jesus Christ, rose from the dead. God's triple star shines over the infinity of the universe. It shines into eternity. It can never be extinguished."

SPHERES

"GOD'S world is divided into different spheres of existence. You on this small planet know only the life on earth and earthly gravity. You can barely imagine a spirit life. But it will not be long before your scientists will have calculated that there is a world of existence, which you can neither see with your eyes, nor bring into focus with your most sophisticated instruments on earth or in space. All souls who have cast off the mortal frame enter this sphere of existence.

"The world of spiritual existence has been created by God in the same way as the world of gravity; it comes from the same essence. Therefore, both creations resemble each other. Nothing has come into being by accident. Imagine the world of heavy matter as being identical with the world of light matter; as identical as an image in a mirror. Your dead live on, bound to reality exactly like you who are still incarnated.

"It is a great error if you imagine the life of the soul to be an existence in dream-like ecstasy, or a state of nirvana into which the spirits sink as into a sea of blissful emotion. The old concept of paradise needs to be rectified, as does the old concept of hell.

"Paradise, in which the good souls are only concerned with being happy, is just as non-existent as hell, in which the evil souls are eternally tortured in a fiery inferno by cruel devils. Mankind is now one stage of development higher than it was a few centuries ago. On the whole, it is not as child-like; it has matured. Therefore, you shall now receive clarification about the spirit world.

"In the course of these reports you will learn what it really looks like in God's flourishing worlds of souls and how people live there. But first, the spheres.

"The earth is surrounded by spheric circles which are very far from one another. In spirit life distances in the universe have no meaning. The cosmic planets resemble the earth in their basic structure. In those spheres closer to the earth are the planets of the shadow-world—the zones of punishment—as well as the planets of purification and soul-cleansing. We have special zones of instruction for the different kinds of human weaknesses and mistakes.

"The ultimate happiness all souls aspire to is to be taken to one of the stars close to God. For us there is no *up* and *down,* but on that sphere most distant from the earth, God's radiance is most powerful. This sphere is called the *highest;* it is the realm of the blessed."

ARCHETYPES OF MAN

"IN YOUR ancient scriptures you read about Adam and Eve and the paradise on earth. From the beginning, life on earth has always been hard, difficult and cruel. But the ancients who received divine revelations, also received the great heritage of memory, of God's memory of a blissful world, a Garden of Eden which he had created in the image of this earth.

"Once God created a man and a woman and awakened them to life: Adam and Eve. These archetypes of man, however, did not live on the earth as you do, but in a spheric spirit world. Paradise with all its creatures was a plan of life for God.

"After this, he began the construction of the earthly world and embarked on the long road of millions of years of disappointments, with anticipations of eternity.

"For the development of the so-called homo sapiens, God utilised soul substance from the Holy Spirit's star current, enriched with soul substance of highly developed animals. It is known in other religions that human souls were formed from highly developed animals as well.

"God stands above all religions. Everywhere God's spirit is at work."

WORLD RELIGIONS AND CHRISTIANITY

"IT IS God's wish that all men on earth shall believe in the Gospels. But believers have insight into the secrets of creation in other world religions too. How much beauty you find in Buddha's teachings! And the great religion of Islam is also a strong source of power for God. The faithful of this community are devout, humble and receptive to the radiations of heaven. All great men of knowledge, all the seers and prophets endowed with divine grace have had special insight into the world beyond. It was not possible, however, to reveal the whole truth to individuals.

"Now is the time for the faithful on earth to unite, in order to combine the great truth, which they all proclaim in their individual religions, into one great religion of love.

"It is totally futile for the initiated to quarrel about minor differences in their religious interpretations. Everybody must respect the opinion of the other man who, in his own way, prays to God and fulfils the laws of humanity. No one should yield to the illusion that he is more knowledgeable, better, or more initiated than the others.

"At all times in the history of mankind very advanced civilisations have existed. All civilisations had their gods, and God has always been the highest, the most sublime spirit, looking down on his creation and influencing it with the currents of heaven as much as he could.

"All great minds have realised that this earthly existence is not the meaning of life. It is also common knowledge that the souls are resurrected and do not remain in their earthly bodies. The ancient founders of religions and their custodians took their tasks very seriously and looked upon the education of their contemporaries as a great necessity. With the knowledge of the soul's eternity, their desire was to better the earthly existence of their fellow men.

"Now you must strive to strengthen the similarity among religions and smooth out minor differences. The age-old arrogance of individuals and communities towards those of a different belief must be stopped.

"These explanations should reassure you in the religious knowledge that you have preserved, but they should also impose strong commandments upon you.

"All you who call yourselves Christians should consider it your common duty to find the right path to unification—the unification of your separate religious groups. Free yourselves from ambition and dogmatism in divine matters. Seek to talk to one another. From the essential insights and principles of the holy scriptures, put together a doctrine that is valid for all believers."

FIVE COMMANDMENTS FOR TODAY

"FULFIL my greatest wish and consider it the first commandment for today: UNITE! Found a league of Christianity and then strive towards a union of world religions! The current of love that flows to God from the non-Christian religions is very strong indeed. Those of a different faith shall keep the great, magnificent temple of love to God on firm foundations; yet they shall recognise that the son of God was on earth in order to redeem all men, to free them from the circle of reincarnation and to make accessible to them the way to a blissful life in God's glorious world.

"None of the communities guarding the heritage of the scribes and the righteous visionaries is safe from the snake-bite of time. The religions of mankind, once firm and well-grounded, have begun to shake and will very soon collapse if no such measures are taken. The Christians are in the greatest danger. Islam and Buddhism have more faithful followers.

"The Christian religion is beginning to lose much ground. One still maintains some of the old traditions, but without believing in the deep truths which this religion contains. For superficial reasons one doesn't dare break away completely, but inwardly one has renounced the faith. Only a few are still aware of the secure shelter which God's love offers. One has nothing more in mind than earthly well-being, a chase after possessions, wealth and luxury. One strives to live as securely as possible, and looks upon this small, short earthly existence as the real life.

Never before as in this century has mankind lived so dependent on itself. It has become a naughty child in puberty; it wants to rid itself of God, as adolescents want to escape their parents' control. It considers itself cleverer than ever before and plunges headlong into disaster.

"But God is a strong and strict Father who does not permit this. His will will enforce a change and the beloved problem child will be called back to the family.

"You should know that you belong to a great, divine family! The supreme head of the family is God, the great lord of the universe. He shines his love out over all forms of life, like a sun. At his side is the son, who was the first to speak to you of God's fatherly love. He is there for all men, in this form of existence as well as in the other. Think of him as your big, holy brother.

"God gave Mary to you as a mother. And you should look upon all star-gods and all angels as exalted relatives, related to you by that tie of love which, originating in God, binds all souls together.

"Strict manners and customs exist in this great family. You who are God's children on earth must feel and express the deepest humility towards all prominent servitors of God. This humility and reverence should also be expressed in gestures. Therefore, my second commandment is: BE HUMBLE!

"Hear now the third commandment: BE STRONG IN YOUR FAITH IN THE GOOD IN MAN!

It is not right if you renounce hope for the improvement of mankind. Those people whose souls are still developing must be improved by the influence of mature and noble souls in such a way that they can begin to eradicate the weakness or the evil within themselves and allow the divine in their souls to begin to develop.

"The gift of the Holy Spirit is in every human being. Never consider a human being lost as long as he lives. Everyone on earth has the possibility of finding his way to God. He is never abandoned. As long as they are still on earth, even the most hardened criminals can hope for an improvement in their degenerate souls. But in most cases they do not succeed on their own. They need the encouragement and the influence of good people.

"All violence committed by men must be stopped. Today's greatest crime is the possession of the ghastly weapons of destruction which are being amassed in the East and the West. Such weapons should not be allowed to exist. They must be destroyed.

"From the hearts of noble people there will be a great storm of indignation against cruelty. So my fourth commandment is: NEVER TOLERATE CRUELTY, INHUMANITY, VIOLENCE and the infliction of pain by the stronger on the weaker!

"Go through life with open eyes and fight with all your might any debasement of human feelings. Consider it your most important duty to work as a protector.

"In today's pharmaceutical laboratories crimes are being committed against living beings in gruesome experiments. There is no way that the infliction of torture can be excused. He who orders it and he who executes it can expect punishment according to the laws of divine justice. Know that these methods of research are of little benefit to man's health. Nature, and the spiritual bond with divine power, offers far superior methods of healing.

"So take as my fifth commandment: PLACE HUMANITY BEFORE ALL OTHER EARTHLY INTERESTS! All interests! Which means that you must overcome the shadows of your earth-bound souls. Learn to disregard filthy lucre. Everyone should live well, according to the level of society to which he belongs, but do not be slaves to money. That which you do not attain in this life will be given to you after your earthly death.

"Live here in the glory of a pure soul and you will experience the love of the angels. They speak to you, they induce thoughts in you, they help you and they make your earthly life better. Go through your earthly fate with these divine companions. Learn to hear their voices: the language of inspiration. Live in their shelter and live for the true life in God's world."

THE EARTH AS A SOUL-FORMING PLANET

"THE earth is exposed to special cosmic radiations. It is the only planet in the whole universe designated to develop the immortal human soul. The stars that are located in visible proximity to the earth all have an influence on this planet, which is positioned close to the sun and which, because of its geological conditions, has rendered possible the great upsurge of life. The radiations on to earth come from currents that flow through the entire cosmos. They are reflected by the stars that surround the earth.

"The earth is a minor, small but infinitely important star in the universe. It gives the cosmos the gift of souls and the gift of life preparation. On it, through God's power, through his spirit and will, life is developed. Life, which then in supreme perfection, lives on in spirit form. This is why this star must not perish.

"The divine rulers who are at home on the stars surrounding you, however, need the power of man's faith to be able to do good. They need the bond of the incarnated souls to the Creator, to God the Lord. They are less powerful when mankind tries to live independently; when it is unaware of the gods, these angels of the stars, all of whom are authorised servants of God. This has happened in this century. A large section of mankind lives without a strong bond of faith and those who do believe are controlled by the narrow-mindedness of the religious community to which they belong.

"Today it must be considered the holiest obligation of man to observe the laws of charity and, in recognition of God on the very highest level, to apply them even to those of a different faith. Very great sins are committed as a result of the arrogance of the members of religious communities. To be a Christian means, firstly to love God. It is exactly the same in the other world religions—the holiest law is the love of God. It is incomprehensible that men who claim to be religious should insult and fight, in the most detestable way, those who belong to a different faith.

"God and Allah are one spirit. And how the unworthy believers behave towards one another! Invoking the holiest name, they commit the most horrendous acts of violence. They cannot imagine what judgment awaits them.

"All men are brethren. All men have been created by the life-forming love of the one great, glorious God, who rules the whole cosmos.

"All men live on this little earth as if marooned on a ship from which there is no escape. If the ship sinks, all are lost. If this were to happen, your happiness of eternal life would be over-shadowed by God's grief over the destruction of the earth, which you would have caused. Therefore, you must first purify your souls. Then the stars will banish disaster and your minds will be inspired by the angels' thoughts which enter. You will then be protected from folly and dangerous reasoning. Ways will be shown to you to preserve the human race, which God will not allow to become extinct, if you commit yourselves to him.

"In the most diverse areas of life restrictions will be imposed upon you. The affluent societies of the industrial nations must revert to a more modest life. The purification of this planet has to be started immediately and carried out with the greatest diligence.

"A global reduction of the birth rate is necessary, because the earth has become too crowded for you. This little planet is congested, worn out and sick. You must now revive it for a future mankind of supreme maturity.

"You will be inspired with all the directions for the preservation of the earth. The pre-condition for this is the starshine of love which you must receive with an open heart. All of you can climb the steep path to the crest of enlightenment. Go with God, my endangered people, and all will be well!"

REINCARNATION

"EARTH is the tree on which the fruits of life ripen, bearing the kernels from which new life blossoms in God's world. Your earthly bodies are only the mortal frames of your souls. If such a frame sickens and the kernel remains healthy, then the suffering is transitory; if, however, the kernel falls sick, the fruit is lost and the tree of life has to bring forth—on the same branch—new fruit which bears a precious kernel. So it is with reincarnation.

"Not only the sick fruits, however, but also those that fall to the ground before they are ripe do not count and must be renewed. But all of you are able to enter God's kingdom without having to live on earth again. The best safeguard against reincarnation is a profound spiritual bond with Jesus Christ. Conform to the teachings of Christianity; there is no better religion for you.

"You who have broken away from the great community of the Church, find your way back to it. Rejoin your brethren who are united in their faith. It is better than being isolated. In this solemn fellowship you are stronger than as an individual.

"If, however, you are not inclined to join one of the Christian communities and you prefer to find the way to God alone, then go out into the star-lit nights when the brilliance of heaven is greatest and offer secret prayers to your Creator. Walk the stony paths of the mountains, in the solitude of the forests, in the silence of nature and dedicate your shining souls to the God of love."

GOD

"YOU humans who turn to God in your prayers should be able to picture him.

"It is written in the Bible that God created man in his own image. Therefore, you know that God's appearance is human. God has a human figure and countenance. He is a personal God and your pantheistic conceptions are based on error.

"His appearance is absolute sublimity, beauty and glory; human, and yet far removed from human in the earthly sense. His countenance is radiant love, holy love, the origin and eternal spring of all love, the eternal life-current of the spirit. In his forehead the energy of the entire universe is closely compacted, the life energy of all that is. The eternal glory of life shines in his countenance. But his eyes, veiled in timeless hope and expectation, still reflect the horror of an era of creation when the powers of chaos raged. This greatest suffering of all, this suffering of many thousand sufferings, which God bears in his soul, will not cease before the Creator's highest hopes have been fulfilled and happiness and peace is given to him by the purity of all souls.

"A heavy shadow still cloaks the Earth, an evil emanation has not yet been extinguished, the aftermath of the storms of creation is still harboured in the souls of many men who are unreceptive to the current of the Holy Spirit. It is only a breath, something which dissolves immediately when men turn their souls to God, when they understand that this most holy tie with God protects them against all the evil of this earth.

"A strong bond of love passes from God into every human heart. It is a current which never fails and which enables even the most evil person to rise up again from the aberrations of life, as long as his heart still beats. Nobody is ever lost, but no sinner on earth can escape from punishment and penance.

"Look up to God! It is his being which causes heaven to flourish. May his glorious heart be your daily shelter. Behold, he is like a man in his feelings. He has determined man's size according to his own stature. God lives as a fully grown man, and so do I, Jesus Christ, and all the angels and all those who are blessed.

"The size of the universe in relation to the human size of God is without any importance, just as the distances in space are no distances for God. His spirit permeates the entire cosmos and with the speed of thought God can reach any place in his infinite kingdom of stars. This is beyond the understanding of you all.

"But now know that God has human feelings; he feels happiness and joy, pain and suffering, disappointment and hope. And he feels a yearning. Yes, his heart constantly yearns for the prayers of your love. All you who are loved by God, let no day go by without thinking of him, without sending him a prayer from the depths of your heart. Pray to him in joy and sorrow and always be aware that this life on earth is only the preparation for the blissful existence in the world beyond. You live here only to mature for the real life."

THOUGHTS AND PRAYERS

"THERE are stars in the universe which have been created only for the purpose of receiving the everyday thoughts of man. These stars are brains of the most sublime construction. They are an invention of God's spirit.

"Thoughts are an expression of the soul. The soul translates emotions into words. Speech is given to you that you may enlighten your consciousness. You do not speak only in order to make yourselves understood, but throughout the day you speak to yourselves. All your emotions are transformed into words. God has designated prominent angels to evaluate your mental soliloquies. When the time comes, your souls are to meet the great expectations of the Holy Spirit; they are to comply with his demands of purity, thereby gaining the bliss of eternal life.

"Thus, according to God's will it has been decreed that human thought be received and that the worth of each individual soul be assessed, examined and judged. A justice of the stars is being meted out to you, a justice which shines in the glory of the Holy Spirit.

"Prayer is a current which differs from the thought-streams of everyday life. Think of it as being like a long-distance telephone call. All those who have learned to pray know the strengthening effect of this current to God. This is not the case for those of you who live completely without faith. One cannot address one's prayers to a God whose personal existence one does not believe in and whose presence one considers impossible.

"But now I want to reclaim all those who have turned away from me. Be released from your torpor! No longer must you walk the stony way of this earthly life alone. Give the ardour of your hearts to the son of God who loves you all!

"It is so simple to pray! A current is there the very moment you prepare a powerful thought within yourselves. It is born in your brains and star currents guide it directly to the Godhead, directly to that divine spiritual force which you invoke. Therefore: your prayers are received in a different way from all your thoughts which concern life on earth. Your prayers enter a holy grail in which they are preserved. Radiant grace is certain for all who pray.

"Oh, do not speak about unfulfilled supplications sent to heaven! Understand that the great decisions of fate cannot always be altered according to your wishes. Be humble and devoted to the Creator, but know too, that much can come to pass through the great power of love, through the strong force of prayer."

THE NATURE OF THE SOUL

"THE people of this century are at the point of exploring the mysterious composition of the soul. Technical photography has succeeded in making visible a duplicate shape around every living being.

"Man strives to uncover the relationship between spirit and matter, but all researchers who try to fathom nature without understanding that it is nothing but God's work are on the wrong path. Their scientific findings—the booty of plunderous research—leaves them bewildered and facing new problems resulting from their discoveries. As much is gained as is lost.

"You will never succeed in exploring nature by means of technology and reason alone. There is only one way to advance—through the bond with God. How many blind alleys you take! Stop exploring the secrets of creation through cruel experiments! Animals are not objects and you must not abuse them by violating all the laws of humanity. Your efforts to penetrate the secrets of God are futile if you do not open the eyes of your soul.

"The soul is a structure comparable to the earthly body. This radiation from God's holy current is given to all creatures. Everything that breathes, therefore every plant, tree and flower, must receive this divine power, otherwise it would fall apart. Call this current in all life *aura, aura Theou*—the breath of God. The more advanced the spiritual development of creatures, the stronger this aura.

"The human soul, however, is of a particular nature. Its inner skeleton is constructed from animal soul-substance, but the divine reflection within comes from a star of the Holy Spirit, which gives birth in the universe to the rays of eternal life like a sun. Your souls are prepared with the greatest love by God's angels. They receive these rays and implant them into the expectant life-form, where they remain until the soul is called to enter a newborn human child.

"Old fairy-tales and legends tell of mysterious appearances of the soul which caused fear to the living. But the senses of the earthly body are generally not able to recognise the phenomenon of the soul. Such recognition is only possible under very special circumstances.

"Souls are the strongest and most stable miracles of life in God's worlds. You imagine them to be of rays, but they have exactly the same bodily appearance as you who live on earth. They detach themselves from the material body, which must perish, but they are also of matter—in a form which you cannot grasp for, as the word expresses, you want to "grasp" in order to understand.

"However, you cannot touch souls, you do not see or feel them and yet they are of a material that is prepared in the same way as your earthly body. But the material is of another composition, of other atoms, of a star-substance sanctified by the eternal Godhead's love of life. The basic structure of the soul is the same as the earthly body in God's sublime conception, but it is made of subtle, spiritual elements.

"The earth is a matter of unique composition, but this matter is nothing other than a web of energy consisting of minute, vibrating particles. Contemporary scientists have already discovered this. It is, therefore, only seemingly solid. Everything is flexibly bound together, held fast by a mysterious power of attraction. What in you is the breath of God—the soul, the aura—exists in every living thing. But in the entire earth and solar system a controlled power of self-attraction causes the binding of matter. This power maintains the shape of all substances. Immortal souls can move through dead matter just as you do through air. Because of this, at the moment of death, the souls of men can be freed from their earthly encasements.

"People can be smashed to death by rocks. They can perish in explosions. The most terrible way of dying today is considered to be destruction by the atomic bomb. But even the bomb cannot destroy the immortal existence of the soul. In whatever way a person dies on earth, his soul lives on and is accepted into the higher realms of spheric life.

"The soul, therefore, is absolutely indestructible. Through earthly life it is formed and strengthened. Even its outward appearance is determined by you. Genetic heritage may give someone an unattractive appearance. But if there is a noble soul within him, his outward appearance is changed when he is freed from his earthly body. His face, which appeared ugly on earth, is transformed in a miraculous way. The disturbances of his incarnate appearance are eliminated in the immortal shape of his soul, in spite of which he is recognised by his loved ones. Those who died before him welcome him in astonishment and joyfully he sees his own image in the mirror. He is changed in a way that has preserved his essential features and has removed only the irregularities of his earthly appearance.

"On the other hand, there are people who on earth were endowed with faces of perfect beauty, but their souls degenerated and, after death they appear so terribly disfigured that they do not recognise themselves. They have to live with that ugly face and body until they have been purified by hard penance.

"You human beings, develop the beauty of your soul through purity of character, through decency and morals, through nobility of the heart and generosity. Recognise your own weaknesses and conquer them!

"Overcome disturbed emotions such as arrogance and pride, vanity, avarice, inconsideration or dogmatism, the exaggerated need for earthly pleasures, for apparent happiness, the numbing of worries through poisons of all kind.

"Remain pure! Never be cold and heartless towards all that needs protection! Attach yourselves to the bonds of love with God with all the power of your hearts—so you will shape the souls within you to perfect beauty."

COSMOS AND LIFE—THE STAR OF PREPARATION

"A LAW of the cosmic spirit compels God to populate his universe with life. Since God is one with the prime spirit of all worlds, this law also sprang from his own soul. It is a necessity. The infinite realms of the cosmic spheres, whose spiritual centre is located within your Milky Way, must be populated with flourishing and prosperous life. The stars

of gravity which you are able to see are only the skeleton of the
gigantic cosmic figure that receives spirit and soul from the souls of
immortality.

"There is a star in the universe created by God only for the
preparation of human souls. It is located within view of your planet
earth, and it is visible due to its core of shining heavy matter. This star
exists both for the creation of new souls and for the purification and
transformation of those who are destined to be reincarnated.

"Human souls evolve from the injection of rays from the current
of life of the Holy Spirit into soul-growths of the earth. In its
original state the human soul is shapeless and the size of a newborn
baby. The resources of expectant life are the most sacred possession of
our God.

"Whenever a sinner from this earth receives the grace of
reincarnation, he is brought to this star of preparation after his penance
and purification. Here there is a river which you may call Lethe. It
flows through the most magnificent landscape you can imagine. Those
who see its waters are overcome by the irresistible desire to drink from
them and bathe in them. It has the purity of a star, the brilliance of a
sun and nobody can bear just to stand in front of it.

"In ecstatic rapture those who have been purified moisten their
hands, foreheads and eyes; they drink and then slip into the holy stream
to bathe. While they bathe, all memory is erased from their souls.
Afterwards they stand amazed, because they have all been beautified.

"Refreshed as well as tired and wrapped in shining white robes
which are gifts from the angels, they are led in a state of dream-like
pleasure to a ship which they board. This ship takes the purified souls
to a place of supreme tranquillity, a building that resembles a Greek
temple. When they enter, they are exposed to the radiation of the glory
and peace of happiness. An angel brings them to a resting place where
they settle down in heavy languor. They are not aware of further
treatment because they fall into a deep sleep.

"In this state they are brought to a different room where, at first, they
remain the size of a human body. But, as their long sleep continues,
their bodies are gradually reduced by exposure to divine rays.
Constantly supervised and cared for, they miraculously attain the form
of the beginning of human life. In this way they lose their external
appearance and finally remain longish, egg shapes in this place of
preparation.

"The guardian angels who looked after them on earth are now anxious to re-awaken their darlings to a new life. This new beginning is determined by the laws of the angels of fate. The guardian angels are notified when the time has come and when the new incarnation—the new cycle of fate—can begin.

"Already at the embryonic stage of earthly life, the angels begin to prepare for the implantation of the soul into the human being. They shine the rays of God's love current on to the developing child. Therefore, it is an act of desecration of the love of God, if you kill unborn children!

"The increase of human beings must be stopped. The making of a child must be considered very carefully. The lovers of this century have the possibility of controlling their relationships; they have birth control. This must be introduced to all nations on earth. In the future there will be new discoveries in this area, for sexual abstinence is, on the whole, not attainable. Nor is it a law of heaven. A law of heaven, however, is love!

"If a little soul is created for you, accept it and let all good gifts from your soul flow into it. The birth of a human being is a great, holy miracle.

"Infinitely more blessed than those destined to reincarnate are those who kept their souls pure and evolved them to maturity. For them there is no stream of oblivion, but rather a life of bliss in God's world; such bliss as you cannot imagine here.

"Realise this: none of you need reincarnate. All of you can enter eternal life. Prove yourselves in this earthly existence. And believe in it in the face of all doubts and temptations: the power of the death of the son of God redeemed you. The gates of heaven are open. Bind yourselves to him who writes you this and who loves you all. Bind yourselves to Jesus Christ."

LOVE AND MARRIAGE—EROS

"EROS is the name of life's prime power. Eros is God's union with all lovers. God gives himself to all souls giving love. He breaks into all hearts aflame with love and his emotion vibrates in all tender, noble souls.

"So man shall give himself to woman only bound by this most

tender power, and may he never weaken her by his compelling wish!

"Enlightened man shall never succumb to the base drive of lust, but without reserve may he complete the union if it is made holy by the harmony of both their souls.

"A strong current which permeates all life is the mysterious attraction between the male and female sex. There is immense power in this drive, which preserves the earthly existence of God's creatures. It is as important as pain for the preservation of life.

"The formation of these absolutely necessary emotions—love and pain—goes back to the dawn of creation. The sexual union of all living creatures is the command of the great, eternal, prime spirit of all worlds. The strong, intoxicating feeling of desire alone makes living beings strive for union, thereby assuring the propagation of all species. Man and animal alike follow a pre-determined, mysterious drive.

"In all generations of the great and glorious ages throughout the history of mankind, love has always been considered a holy gift from heaven. Poets of all times have sung of the thoughts and feelings of happy lovers; of the yearnings, torments and joys of love. Generations have come and gone, and love has always flowed through life with the same power. Oh, human beings, rejoice in this great, divine gift of God.

"But reach for the star-like brilliance of love through the soul's sacred emotions before you surrender to the bliss of union. See how God's great tenderness flows through all creatures. Enjoy each other as you love each other. Give each other everything your hearts possess in the way of tender feelings. Be unafraid as you give yourselves completely. God loves you and if the sweet feelings of your senses are pure, they will never appear as sins in the world of stars.

"You humans all have a very sensitive feeling for what is good and what is evil. All you who love, obey the voice of your conscience and the law of your heart. The stars of love rise above every couple who preserves the soul's purity.

"The purity of the soul is very necessary; without this pre-requisite, the blessed current of heaven cannot be acquired, this current from the stars which allows lovers every liberty. God's angels are very strict in the examination and judgement of soul values. They are the guardians of decency and morality. They punish aberrations of sensuality which stray beyond the normal relationship between man and woman to sexual perversion. They punish already on earth.

"There are the most disgusting aberrations of primitive sensuality which I am not inclined to discuss further. There are people who transgress the limits of human dignity in their sexual desires and try to capture sensual pleasures in a manner that exceeds the feeling of shame. You must observe the feeling of shame when you surrender to the body's desire for sensual enjoyment, for it is this feeling that keeps you from sexual aberrations. If you are not able to sense this shame within you, then you have come to a very low level. You have sunk below the meaning of the word: human being. This abnormal greed for sensual pleasure is incompatible with the dignity of man.

"Sensuality is divinely ordained. The currents of Eros pervade the whole earth, the whole world. They permeate the cosmos up to the highest spheres of life. The currents of Eros, however, are pure.

"Love and tenderness are the sweetest feelings of divine life. The love-power of sensuality which is ignited by the desire and the joy of female beauty and of male strength is a wonderful gift from God which you may enjoy freely. But never follow the ways of corruption. Never let yourselves be seduced to seek the ecstasy of the senses in a way that desecrates the holy treasure of the soul.

"And finally a word for the present time. Due to popular sex education to which even little children are exposed, today's young people have lost certain natural restraints. They indulge in the sensation of complete freedom in the enjoyment of love. On the whole, however, they still strive for the happiness of a deep, emotional love.

"It shall be noted: sexual liberation must not transgress the limits of decency and the morals of the social order of a civilised human race. An aberration into total sexual freedom causes mankind a great loss of spiritual values. Therefore, the young must be cautioned to moderation. They must be warned not to regard sensual desires as the most important aspect of life.

"The search for a life-time companion—a companion whose soul is in harmony with one's own—shall still be the goal of youth. Playing around, and thoughtlessly, superficially drifting from one relationship to another means a substantial decrease in soul value.

"Furthermore, marriage shall remain an insoluble bond of love for life. It is a holy promise before God. But really unhappy marriages may be dissolved; for God's most important law is that humanity must prevail.

"You must not burden this earthly existence with contentious conditions. Make the best of every day! Oh, how much time you waste

by making each other's lives miserable. Live in peace! God desires
the harmony of hearts and souls. Live in peace and you will give joy
to God.

"Surrender yourselves into God's hands together, you who truly and
deeply love each other and his love will lighten your way; his glory
will shine over your life and the wonderful feeling of security given to
you by your guardian angels will be transmitted to your children,
whom you shall raise according to the great, holy principles of the
Christian religion and the laws of high ethics.

"Marriage is sanctified, but it is only sanctified through love. If love
dies in a marriage, if all feeling of belonging together is extinguished,
this marriage saddens God, because it is a lie. Such a lie shall not be
continued. God forgives the aberrations of the heart, but continuous
lying is a heavy sin. The worst breach can be healed if a marriage is
basically sound. Strive to step in front of the altar as mature people,
knowing the weaknesses of your chosen partner.

"All ways on earth lead you through light and shadow. It is in the
happiness of the love you give that you find God's blessing."

ABOUT CHILDREN

"AT BIRTH every child has a pure soul, but it has to develop it.
Through the particular life into which it has been placed, it must build
and advance this pure soul to the highest level. If the child fails, its
soul is cleansed and reincarnated and is pure once again at the outset.

"If the child's fate places it in a life that gives it the possibility of
fulfilling God's laws and it does not act accordingly, it has failed. If a
child develops in such a way that its soul remains pure, if it pays
attention to its conscience and suppresses all the bad qualities which
could develop, it will readily enter heaven.

"Parents, always believe in the good that is in your children! It is
possible that a child becomes involved in a crisis; if so, give it all the
more love. If, through foolishness or weakness it has done wrong, do
not punish it too severely. Help it back on to the right path. Should it
occur, however, that a child commits an inhuman and brutal deed, it is
in serious danger.

"Implant into the hearts of your children as soon as they begin to
think and understand, the love of all God's creatures. Children who

love animals will never be able to be cruel. Never permit your children to torture animals or abuse them through thoughtless neglect.

"Explain to them that all animals, even the smallest ones, can feel pain and are not toys. A person who already as a child loved God's creatures will always have reverence for creation and as an adult will have compassion for his fellow men.

"Even if a child is born into a miserable life, its soul will mature. You have all suffered at one time or another, or you are doing so now, or you will do so in the future.

"The apparent injustice of eathly fates is only so from man's point of view. According to the highest order, there is no injustice. Every soul can prove itself in this life and mature to perfection.

"For those who were raised as Christians and remain bound to God's son in their life on earth, there is no reincarnation. They enter God's world."

HOW ONE SHOULD LIVE

"LET the purity of the soul be your highest goal. God's world is open to all those who die with a pure heart and a pure soul. It is open to believers as well as unbelievers. There are people who are unable to believe, but who live an exemplary life and are noble-minded and magnanimous. They compensate God for their unbelief by the purity of their souls. On the other hand, the gates of heaven remain shut to believers who fail as human beings.

"Every one of you feels in your soul the current of God that enables you to distinguish between good and evil. Your conscience, that most subtle sense within you, tells you immediately whenever you act against God's will. Never numb your conscience by thoughts and acts of egoism.

"Live in a way that brings joy to God. Always be aware of the fact that all your thoughts are being heard. Be decent in life and noble in mind. Always behave in such a way that the good deeds of your life—thrown on to the scales—far outweigh your shortcomings. Take care that in your life you never commit an evil action that cannot be atoned for. Deep repentance can improve your soul, but it is difficult to expiate a wicked deed.

"Do not think that at the end of your life you simply have to confess and repent your evil deeds in order to enter eternal bliss. The laws concerning the purity of souls, the quality of the psychic substance which you are supposed to have achieved here by the end of your lives, are much stricter. And the power of the angels of fate who guard you is great.

"You have no idea how much you do wrong. You constantly strive for riches. All the time you are trying to improve your earthly lives, but you do not think of improving yourselves. Live this life of preparation with the greatest reverence for creation and the deepest humility for God's grandeur.

"Many thousand pathways lead to God. Let each one of you fortify your soul in prayer, so that you do not fail to find the one destined for you."

THE EVIL IN MAN

"EVER since mankind has believed in God it has also believed in an antagonist of God. The belief in a spirit of evil developed already in the first natural religions. This spirit of evil had many names, just as God had many names. The Bible tells the story of the angel Lucifer whom God cast out. And in the New Testament there are some references to Satan. Through the belief in Satan and the fear of the machinations of this evil spirit, great misfortune befell mankind in the Middle Ages.

"At this time God was deeply distressed by the cruelties committed in the name of the cross. In his disappointment that Christians in their religion were capable of committing the most terrible deeds, he came close to obliterating Christendom in these centuries. You know how the plague decimated populations. This sickness was a quiver of God's soul, but a simultaneous upsurge in the veneration of Mary moved the Father's heart to pity. Know that the end of the plague was due to the love of Mary. The strong current of glowing love from thousands of human hearts to Mary gave God new hope for the awakening of a superior and noble Christianity in a later age.

"In the striving for perfection there is a strong polarity of evil and good. In the shaping of the divinely sublime there is the resistance of matter, the resistance of the elemental powers of nature.

"God is the greatest moulder. What he created from nothing is immense, and to produce order from chaos he had to overcome the resistance of a cosmos. He also had to undertake the great task of repressing the evil in man in order to win over more and more good souls. God has constantly to do an enormous amount of work, so that everything remains within the laws of order and that which has been brought to order does not revert to chaos.

"God also works extensively for the preparation of human souls. Chaos is the original condition of all matter and chaos lies in your souls too. Only because of the constant radiation of God's spirit do you humans progress along the path of righteousness.

"A host of guardian angels lives only for you. Very many angels of fate work constantly to make you more perfect. The way to perfection is long!

"Man tends to attribute all evil on this earth to the very strong influence of Satan. You must now understand the old concepts of hell and purgatory differently. And you must also alter your idea of the devil.

"It is not as you used to believe. God is the sole ruler of the eternal and infinite cosmos. He has overcome the spirit of evil, which is symbolised as a dragon or a serpent in the Revelations of St John. In these writings I cannot give you exact explanations of everything. These are the most secret matters. The spirit of evil is an immense element which you must not confine to Satan as a person.

"The great movements of the universe, which God first had to shape, had to be forced to order by the strongest will. Consider this resistance of a living cosmos, which represented chaos in opposition to the power of order, as "the spirit of evil". Through my human incarnation, my death and my resurrection, God triumphed over the spirit of evil, the cosmic resistance to his holy work.

"The whole universe has been purified. It has become strong and healthy.

"Now it is up to you human beings to exterminate the evil in your souls. Each one of you can overcome the "devil". You have your conscience, you know exactly what is good and what is evil. Conquer the evil! Bind yourselves to God and the word: Satan will be forgotten in a new age.

"Know that everybody who commits evil here has to account for it. Nobody is able to excuse himself for having committed an evil deed by blaming the devil for leading him astray. Everyone stands alone at the last judgment. The judges of God are strict and just. The hardened sinners who do not repent face dire punishment. However, they are not thrown into a flaming inferno by a devil; instead are guided to their punishment by the angels of the world of shadows.

"We have a sphere of punishment—the world of shadows. The sinner is first punished at the place of his crime and then he is brought to the world of shadows, which is what you call "hell".

"The lord of the shadow world is a powerful, handsome, independent star-god and therefore, an angel of fate. His name is Phosphoros, but also Lucifer. He works for God. He has a difficult task to fulfil and rules over a large number of angels who are separate from the angels of light. They are very serious, distinctively dressed angels. They wear dark, silver-shimmering robes.

"Every marked person—a sinner who bears the mark of Cain—sees, after his death, such a dark angel standing next to his guardian angel, who is of light and radiant beauty. The guardian angels of criminals and sinners are very, very sad when they have to hand over their human children to one of these important angels of the shadow world. So Phosphoros, like fate-empowered Saturn, is in the service of God and his task is the punishment of sinners.

"It may occur that you feel inclined to do evil and believe yourselves to be under the influence of Lucifer. The evil, however, lies solely within yourselves. A good person can never be induced to commit an evil deed. As soon as you succumb to evil and burden yourselves with heavy sin, the mark of Cain is drawn on your forehead by an angel. Now only the deepest repentance, combined with the most ardent prayers for pardon can save you.

"God tests you. God's angels of fate often impose heavy burdens on your shoulders. You are also led into temptations by dark powers, but it is easy for you to pass all tests and resist all temptations.

"God wants his souls to be strong; strong and unchallengeable. He tempers his severity with love. You are to live eternally! You must not be susceptible to sin, to decadence, to all earthly, tempting influences that are inferior and superficial. Wealth is also a test and in no way a reward! You will only be rewarded in heaven. According to God's will, hard-heartedness is bitterly punished in the world of shadows by the lord of those realms.

"Everyone of you is bound to God's heart by a cord of love. God loves all his people. Even the worst sinner should remember this in his weakest hour.

"God grants you great mercy through the bond of thought with him. This is the grace of prayer. Every prayer is heard, even if your wishes cannot always be fulfilled.

"Prayers are like long-distance telephone calls; they are always heard. God, or that spirit power of God which you call upon, always receives your words and always has time for you. Pray! Send your thoughts to heaven. Talk to your guardian angels, call upon Mary or your saints and those powers of fate whom you meet in these writings. They are great, strong and glorious angels of God and all love you!

"God has conquered the original power of resistance. *You* have to conquer the evil within you. Whoever is firmly convinced that there is no death will never again dare to commit evil.

"Everyone should live and act in such a way that he may behold God after his earthly life. Everyone should defeat the evil within himself and bind himself firmly to God's great bond of love which connects heaven and earth. And the day will come when God will be able to assign different, heavenly tasks to his dark angels.

"We do not await the end of the world; we await an age of divine fulfilment, an age of man who goes through life nobly and decently; who knows of God's great miracles and the endless love the Father gives him. Think no more of the destruction of the earth. Obey the laws of heaven and you will go towards a glorious future."

THE WORLD OF SHADOWS AND THE MATURATION OF SOULS

"EVERY person who committed evil on earth enters the shadow world. He remains completely locked in his personality. His punishment is exactly in accordance with his evil deeds. There are the most varied punishments, just as there are the most varied crimes and sins. Never has a sinner been condemned to eternal damnation. Everyone has the chance to climb up from the world of darkness into the higher realms of light. Everyone is granted the great, divine mercy of penance.

"Penance has to be endured in the world of shadows until the soul has been purified. Since there are gruesome souls—people who commit the most dreadful cruelties—there is also gruesome pain and suffering in the shadow world. The souls have to endure exactly the same pain they inflicted on other people or on animals.

"We have people in the shadow world who—measured in earthly time—are exposed for centuries to unfeeling spirits who inflict upon them the measure of suffering they have deserved. But even these people, who are kept in a state of great physical pain and mental anguish, stand on the steps of development. Even from the very bottom step there is a way back to the light—through life on earth. There is no eternal damnation. Pain and suffering without end does not exist.

"The concept of a hell in which men lie in torment for eternity has its origins in inaccurate translations. This will be scientifically clarified by a re-examination of the first records of the Holy Scriptures.

"In due course the punishment of every soul is ended and the person is left to the influence of special teachers. Angels who are physicians of the soul now deal with him. They hope for a great catharsis and a dawning of realisation in the watching mind; watching, because all his crimes and cruelties are shown to him in picture form. God waits a long time for the human mind to understand.

"If this does not occur, if a heart remains cold, then such an extremely ugly soul is not pardoned to reincarnate as a human being. It is disposed of, in that it is returned to the original life form of earth. As a human soul it is extinguished. God only sends back its immortal element to begin anew on earth. And once again it is guided through the same preparations which mark the long path of evolution for all souls.

"Like all things that are meant to attain perfection, souls must mature. They have to achieve a great increase in value in their evolution. Every soul is destined to enter God's great world one day. But in God's world only the most noble souls can find entry. Therefore, reincarnation is a necessity. Punishment for evil deeds is also a necessity. It is a mercy for those who have been evil that they are punished, for this is the only way for their souls to be saved.

"Punishment is conducted in such a way that brings great increase to soul value. A person who was cruel in this life will never again be cruel after the punishment he has had to suffer.

"Everyone marked with the sign of Cain undergoes a strict examination. His way of life is carefully scrutinised and all circumstances that led to his crime are discussed. Everything that can be considered in his defence is taken into account. The very highest justice and wisdom of God is evident in the manner in which the punishment is carried out.

"Good people with only minor faults immediately enter a beautiful, bright world where they are educated in a wonderful way. This education is conducted by the angels of God. They are those angels who, as guardian angels, already looked after their human children on earth. Now, in the loving, but strict, fashion that characterises them, they attend to the maturation and development of their charges.

"Minor sinners can therefore be certain that they will not be thrown into purgatory. Instead they will be educated. If you demonstrate good will, you will even be allowed to meet your relatives and friends. The joys of meeting again are delightful. However, immature souls are, on no account, allowed to visit mature souls. Only the reverse is possible. The spirit beings who are more advanced descend to those who have not progressed so far. They tell about their home and bring to their beloved, anxiously awaited ones, the radiance of a blissful world."

A WARNING TO EVERYONE

"YOU shall all be blessed one day when you have passed the test of life on earth, but what difficulties, what dangers stand in your way!

"It is very easy to satisfy the demands of the deputies of God. A German poet expressed it very simply:
"Man should be noble
Helpful and good"
"How natural it should be to live accordingly! All who follow this rule are flourishing boughs on the tree of eternal life whose trunk is firmly rooted in the religions. They are the life-absorbing roots of a mankind blessed to rise from the regions of gravity to the realms of celestial bliss, to the joys of star-lit, eternal life. It is God you must recognise while living on this earth, you who are spiritually blind!

"I want to redeem you, but only the purification of your mind enables me to do this. Your mind is endangered, for you deem yourselves more knowledgeable than all generations before you. You have developed one-sidedly.

"I want to eliminate the icy currents that have penetrated your brains. The earth, on which you potter around, is doomed. The earth is dying and if you do not listen to me, it will be the end. There is no generation in human history that has ravaged this beautiful planet the way you have! You are sick in mind and soul, because you have broken away from God.

"Oh, you lords of the industrial nations, you fill my soul with horror! You mighty of this earth, how you make me shudder! You are insane in the soullessness of your godless existence. This earth is a jewel in the universe. A jewel! And you are destroying it!

"God has created eternally blooming, sunny realms among the stars for you—you who have only been given earthly bodies, so that you may evolve and prove yourselves—worlds of a beauty that you cannot imagine. You shall live in bliss without pain, without death, to the delight of God who loves you more than words can say. But here you exist in your conceit, in your limitless stupidity, greedy for power and money, building the most dreadful weapons of destruction with your god-forsaken brains, penetrating the secrets of nature without the slightest respect and not knowing how deathly miserable are the souls within you.

"Bristling with violence, the super-powers face each other and threaten the peace of the world. They are dominated by ideas of conquest and strong feelings of power, but they will never achieve their aims. An upsurge of faith from within will sweep through all nations. There is a deep longing for faith in the hearts of millions of troubled Christians.

"You must grow strong in your faith, strong in your bond with God, but strong also in the face of threats and attacks. Nevertheless, be prepared at all times to extend the hand of friendship should your opponents listen to reason. Never forget, you are all brethren in the presence of God. Keep hatred at bay! Always be ready to forgive, always be ready to love, always be ready to recognise your opponents and convince them through the power of the spirit, the power of the word. Defend the property of human freedom against every attack but, at the same time, always preserve the heart's power of faith in the good in man, even in the enemy.

"Behold, this earth still smoulders. Mankind is preparing great sorrow for itself in its ungodliness. But from the terrible happenings of the present time the way will point mankind to a blissful future.

"There is one means of rescue for all of you. It is in the soul of every individual. Bind yourselves to God! Open your hearts to your maker in humility and love. Only an open vessel can be filled. You can receive God's radiations from all the stars above you. Take them!"

SUPPLEMENTS AND EXPLANATIONS OF THE HOLY GOSPELS

"MY soul desires to supplement and explain the writings of the Gospels in several places. Gaps in the memories of the evangelists and minor errors of translation have made it necessary to correct some passages from the New Testament.

Matthew 10-34/40
"Think not that I am come to send peace on earth: I came not to send peace, but a sword.

"For I am come to set a man at variance against his father, and the daughter against her mother, and the daughter-in-law against her mother-in-law. And a man's foes shall be they of his own household.

"He that loveth father or mother more than me is not worthy of me: and he that loveth son or daughter more than me is not worthy of me."

"These were not my words. I said: "I have not come to calm the world, I have come to arouse it. You who belong to me and believe in me, acknowledge me, wherever you are. Acknowledge me and do not renounce me. If, in your family you are alone in your belief, fight with the sword of the word from your heart's conviction for the truth of my teaching. Fight even—should it be necessary—against father and mother, sister and brother, against all your household, until their unbelief has been overcome.

"Nobody loves you more deeply than I. If you return my love, I will reward you for it on the day you stand before the Father. Follow me! I lead you along the right path. Be strong in your soul, every one of you, for I am with you.

"Prove to me that you are worthy of my love. I give you more than father and mother, son and daughter are able to give you. Whosoever receives me, receives him who sent me and his reward is certain.

"This was the sense of my words. I preached very many things, but my basic thoughts were along these lines.

"The Sermon on the Mount has essentially been well and properly recorded, but I would add that it was much richer in content.

Matthew 5/3
"Blessed are the poor in spirit, for theirs is the kingdom of heaven."
"This sentence must be explained: the thoughts of intellectuals are

dangerous, because they distract from pure feeling. You must preserve purity of feeling! If you seek to penetrate the secrets of creation soley with reason, you do not pave your way to God. Should you have been given a sharp mind and the faculty to think clearly, you will miss the good, simple pathway to God, if you do not allow your soul to move in harmony with the spirit.

"Reason is often in conflict with the simple intuition of feeling. A sharp intellect is no match for instantaneous apprehension.

"The statement 'Blessed are the poor in spirit' has a deeper significance. It does not mean that stupidity is an admission ticket to heaven. But you should all preserve the simplicity of your feelings. The simple, straightforward belief in God which seeks no explanation is a strong invigorator of the heart. No pros and cons should stand in the way of this elementary, sure emotion.

"Blessed are they that mourn, for they shall be comforted."

"I will tell you the meaning of this saying. The highest grace of heaven is experienced by those who suffer misfortune and maintain a pure heart. If you have an earthly life of misery and misfortune and still preserve the purity of your soul in deep humility of heart, then your suffering will be compensated a thousandfold in heaven by the most magnificent joys.

"If you are harmed by a harsh destiny on earth, if something terrible happens to you, if you belong to those afflicted by the severest disasters, but your soul maintains the strong bond of trust in God, then the most glorious gifts will be yours as soon as you are able to leave this earth.

"The love radiance of God is in everyone's heart. Nothing happens that glorious God does not see. Give yourselves to him in joy and in sorrow and you will enter eternal bliss.

"You see, for some of the ways of destiny there is no earthly remedy. There are misfortunes that simply have to be accepted. Think of those of your sisters and brothers who endure the hard fate of severest physical handicap. Think of those who have had to surrender to blindness, those fallen victim to leprosy, those born with incomplete bodies, those for whom a severe calamity has destroyed the great, burgeoning joy of life. You see, the path across earth lies in shadow, but it leads to the light of eternal bliss.

"Those who suffer are comforted in a way that the tenderest lover cannot imagine. Show your God the purity of your soul and your heart's deep attachment to Jesus Christ and even in the most severe suffering you will feel the flow of grace. In heaven however, God's love will compensate in the most wonderful way for all earthly suffering.

"Blessed are the meek, for they shall inherit the earth."

"This saying can be misunderstood. I emphasised meekness, which injects the heart's tender feelings into the formation of thought. I placed my trust in people who do not brutally jerk the reins of the bridle towards themselves. I relied on people in whose souls the radiance of gentleness lies. This was my idea. They were to be more powerful than those who wanted to conquer the world with brutal, destructive actions.

"The earth belongs only to him who knows how to understand it in his heart. The beauty of the world is visible only to him who absorbs it into his soul. It is not important how much you have seen on this earth, but how you have seen it. Blessed therefore are the sensitive, for they possess the kingdom of the earth.

"All the remaining sentences of the Sermon on the Mount do not require further explanation."

THE DECAY OF CULTURE

"A NEW human race shall arise for you do not constitute God's highest goal. You are a building that is crumbling away; a rotten, worm-infested, decaying construction in the urban panorama of the divine world. I would almost be inclined to let you go under, because you have earned nothing better.

"You were created as divine beings with many possessions, with the experience of millenia. You live in the existing order of an inherited culture. You are endowed with spirit and intelligence. You behold the eternal light of the stars and the sun's rays shine upon you. You live as free, thinking, knowing people—and abandon yourselves to destruction!

"You are already in such a state of decay that the gods considered letting you sink down into total ruin. But the powerful star-angels are bound to the command of God's son.

"I will strengthen your souls and stop the horrifying events of this process of destruction. I will prevent the disaster of the end of the world, which you have provoked. You will not be wiped out in the horror of nuclear wars. God's son will rescue the dying earth for the Father. See in this a fulfilment of prayer. A prayer of despair coming from the souls of the blessed, from billions of angel and human souls penetrated God's kingdom of stars. It was "SAVE THE EARTH!" The spirit of the cosmos gives his grace, the son of God gives the power of his love and the star-angels, guided by divine decree, are now counteracting the drift into global decline with all their might.

"You see that God's love and mercy are stronger than the justice of the stars, which would let you proceed along the trail to destruction that you have blazed for yourselves. You have not deserved such mercy, you people of this century, but the whirlpool of aberration is not yet strong enough to have swept you all away. The noble souls among you, who tower over the mass of weak and inferior beings, return the reflection of divine love to heaven. They are those on earth who have understood the truth and whom God's son chooses to enlighten others. I want to enlighten you my people!

"Pay attention now: you will witness a mighty struggle for purification. We notice a multiple glow of yearning in many hearts that long for the creation of a different, better, simpler and more natural life; that long for harmony and beauty and for protection in the love of God. A desire of these searchers is the redeemer's appearance on this desolate earth. *And this has occurred!*

"With all my might, oh my people, I will work for the salvation of the earth and for the improvement and bliss of your souls.

"This book is only a beginning. All those who believe that there is no God will, against the fundamental attitude of their minds, be convinced that they have been mistaken. Their enlightenment will bring forth love, and love will save the earth.

"The gods are aghast at the disillusionment and coldness of your souls. You are the inheritors of a sacred culture, and you make available to the invading force of a minority—who operate on mankind like a cancerous ulcer—every means for the execution of their destructive activity.

"What you have owned and what you have brought to flower has not yet faded, it has not died; its development is only hampered by rank weeds. It is the high time that you call to mind the gifts heaven has conferred upon you. Do not go through life as distorted images. The star-gods are horrified to see how you favour the spirits of decline.

Indifference, stupidity and insecurity is your only reaction to this systematic destruction of culture, which you are all able to recognise as the expression of a sickness of mind and soul, as an insult to the divine laws.

"Never has a destructive mind been influenced by the soul of an angel. It is impervious and deaf to the suggestions of its guardian angel. Such a mind recruits the material for its self-presentation from its own baseness. It offers to you the deviations of its restricted brain as a manifestation of human "culture" and "art" with the sole purpose of defrauding you.

"My people, build again a healthy, flourishing and wonderful world bound to God!"

EARTHLY DEATH AND RESURRECTION

"FEAR of death is a law of nature, therefore it is a holy law of the cosmic spirit. This immense fear of dying is necessary for the preservation of earthly life. It is implanted in all creatures as a force to preserve the species. The glowing urge to live results in the acceptance of all the troubles of life.

"You must consider your earthly life the most important and the most precious gift from God. You must never damage, through neglect, the body which envelops the soul. Recognise in this earthly existence the good fortune of being able to prepare the soul for the inconceivable miracle of resurrection. Know that you are to await, with the utmost anticipatory joy, this supreme happiness of a new life the moment your souls are released from your lifeless bodies.

"Nobody who knows his soul to be pure should fear death any longer! You who are old or sick, await the inevitable end with the greatest calm and willingness. Do not cling desperately to this earthly life. See, you are only taking off a cloak that has enveloped you. Death is nothing more.

"You who have lived according to God's laws, your souls are filled with radiance when you awake and open your eyes. You look into a countenance of wonderful, heavenly beauty and you recognise your angel in his magnificent, glorious appearance. His arms embrace you tenderly and, filled with his love, you feel a supreme happiness that even I am unable to describe.

"You people, look forward to dreaded death with the greatest joy!

"God's son has risen from the dead and has prepared the way for all of you.

"To die is the beginning of life. To die is only a shadow that leads to the light. To die is the most gentle awakening in the arms of an angel, the most blissful recognition of God's love, the supreme joy of resurrection."

ETERNAL BLISS

"YOU people hear much about supreme happiness in heaven. It seems very conceivable to you that souls live on in a world of light, but the joy of eternal life was God's most difficult creation. For happiness is like light. Only because of shadow does one recognise the beauty of light: only through contrast, the form of what exists, the shape of all things. Therefore, God's intense love is not possible without discipline and eternal life is not possible without law and order.

"The world beyond has been constructed with supreme wisdom. Selected angels of the stars were entrusted by God with the task of preparing and preserving the order of state which is the foundation of eternal life, the fundamental condition of an existence which cannot be ended by death. This order has been scheduled in the most wonderful way.

"Seraphim stand in the service of the Creator as illustrious rulers of human souls. They build and preserve the eternal happiness of man. But the waxing of happiness is only possible where work brings radiance into hearts, where tasks have to be accomplished and where there is variation. A monotonous existence in idleness would be unbearable over a lengthy period of time, even in paradise.

"It is the great task of the angels to invigorate the lives of men. They are rulers of fate in the world beyond, creators of individual destinies in a place where there is no suffering and no danger.

"Time, in the world beyond, is quite different from here. Time is a concept which implies a beginning and an end. We have only a beginning, the birth as it were into this world beyond, but no limitation of time. There is nothing to terminate life and consequently the redeemed are blissfully calm and serene. But this knowledge of total security would have a very adverse effect on people if they were left to their own devices. They would make one another's lives unbearable through ill-humour if they had nothing else to do but be eternally happy. Happiness is comparable to light, which requires the polarity of shadow.

"Therefore, you must understand that God's seraphim are very, very necessary for people's happiness in life. They ensure that everybody is constantly watched over, just as they are here. But you must not imagine this to be a totalitarian kind of control of the souls, as is described in utopian stories. Rather it is an observance of love that is bestowed on people in the world beyond. Should feelings of fatigue accompany inner changes, diversion is provided by the withdrawal of what has been customary. This is in accordance with higher laws. Fates are guided, relationships altered, tasks modified and purifying re-adjustments effected.

"You must see it like this: the soul is a complete replica of the body. Every cell of the earthly body is embedded in the body of the soul. The soul lies within your earthly body like a structure of rays. Unless this basic soul structure is integrated into your physical body you would be unable to live. So it is that all the functions of the earthly body are taken over into the life of the world beyond. Life in God's state is lived in an entirely human, natural and realistic way.

"The world beyond is provided with the same inter-relationship of elements as the earth. Therefore we also have a wonderful flora and fauna in heaven. But with this difference: the animals in the world beyond exist without the necessity of killing one another. The animals on earth are soul-forming archetypes out of which the happy species of the forms of life of the other world evolve. These divine thoughts of the Creator exist in an immense variety of species in the life beyond and they are not bound by the earthly laws of nature.

"You see, the creation of earth had to conform to earthly conditions of life. In the world beyond God has quite different possibilities of preserving and ensuring the happiness of the animals taken from this world. Cats, for instance, which regard mice as their toys and eat them on earth, are just as lovely and playful in the world beyond. But they do not play with living beings. Instead they play with things, which flourishing nature gives them to maintain their joy of life.

"God has created an enchanting world of a many thousand wonders—a world sparkling in the spheric shimmer of beauty, in which he included the animal world. Through God's love of life, many marvels are prepared for men and animals in the world beyond.

"There all creatures are fed by nature, which blooms and thrives in a profusion which God could not create in the world of heavy matter. And only in your most magical dreams could you imagine a nature which produces the most magnificent, re-invigorating fruits in such infinite variety.

"For man's pleasure the animal world is incorporated into the environment of the bright spheres. Earthly impulses, like the inclination to hunt and kill, no longer exist in human souls. Animals live there to delight by their grace and beauty, affection and love, playfulness and high spirits and to give the human souls the realisation of the unity, inter-dependence and solidarity of all creation.

"The bliss of eternal life is provided and secured by the order of state of the angels. The whole of the world beyond is subject to this order. Earth-like confusion does not exist. In many areas these worlds have been built by man himself. This is a retrospect of history. The earth-like realms of the blessed have been magnificently constructed by generations of human beings who have advanced from the earth to these spheres. And so mankind is given sites of remembrance of all ages.

"A great miracle of the stars is the secret of God's memory. Divine thoughts never perish. Therefore, in the spheres there are cities of the earth from classical antiquity, even from pre-historic cultures.

"We also have the miracle of the light-reflection of all divine thoughts in the celestial substance of eternal construction.

"Nothing that has sprung from God's spirit is ever lost. The past of the earth is ever-lasting present. The blessed are released from time.

"Blissful life is an existence in beauty. Eternity is motion without time.

"Time is linked to an end, to decline, to death. We have no end, no death. Therefore, time dissolves in eternity. What remains is motion, for nothing stands still.

"God's spirit is stimulation. This stimulation permeates everything. If the whole universe of stars did not receive the vibrations of God's power, all life would become inert.

"The blessed, therefore, live in timelessness, wonderfully stimulated and continuously refreshed by divine impulses. But even in the realm of stars of the world beyond, the hours pass. The stars do not stand still. Heaven pulsates in the rhythm of eternity.

"A time current of steady stimulation flows through the universe. It is like an inhalation and exhalation of the cosmos. All life beyond is subject to this rhythm. So the threads of history extend through life in the even pace of motion. Life tasks are fulfilled, new ones set and fulfilled again. There is constant motion.

"In the world beyond suns also shine on the planets. Variation is brought about by periods of proximity and remoteness so that, even in the environment of the blessed, there is winter and summer.

"Beauty is created wherever God is active. Behold how beautiful God's creatures are on earth, incorporated into the conditions of earthly existence! How beautiful is the appearance of time-bound creatures, inheritors of the Creator's wonderful ideas! When they enter the realms of eternal life, they are released from all time-bound imperfections.

"Although the blessed wanderers through eternity shine in the glory of God, they are, nevertheless, under the strict command of his will. God's will is the supreme law.

"All people, whether in this world or in the world beyond, are watched over. A comprehensive picture of the soul of every man on earth is obtained from the constant observation of his thoughts, his words and his deeds. "God hears and sees everything" is not a fairy-tale for children; it is reality. So it is that the worthiness or unworthiness of the soul is crystallised by the observation and examination of the entire life-span.

"The blessed enter heaven as redeemed souls of high spiritual value. There, they are no longer examined for worthiness or unworthiness. They are redeemed for all times—freed from reincarnation. They live independently and without restraint. Nobody troubles them with instructions, although the vibrations of their hearts are watched. These vibrations are registered by special receivers. This is a type of health inspection of the soul.

"If a person's soul is burdened and his emotions register signs of disturbance, there is intervention in his life. The qualities endangering his happiness are illuminated, and law-giving angels step in.

"A strong bond of love unites all who live in the world beyond and yet it is possible for happiness to become endangered. Signs of fatigue can cloud the state of propinquity; feelings of weariness from habitual activities can arise and so on. In such cases strict divine justice affords renewed happiness of life by withdrawing the customary pleasant conditions and leading the person back to the light through shadow. The arrangements made by the angels are not even noticed. Circumstances and events influenced by fate refresh and invigorate life.

"God's love and God's wisdom is above everything man has ever been able to understand and imagine."

STARS—GODS—ANGELS

"THE relationship of time and eternity is similar to the relationship of the stars of heavy matter and the stars of spiritual existence. You can determine events in galactic development; you measure light years; with your eyes you see events that took place millions of years ago; you recognise the new formation and the disintegration of stars; and from everything that you understand, you conclude that the cosmos is expanding with immense speed.

"What you are able to observe is the heavy body of the universe. You do not see the soul of the universe, the spirit world of existence. It is built into the body of the cosmos, as the soul into the body of earthbound man. It is the spirit world that you must now reconcile with the visible world.

"Thousands of years ago an ancient human race learned that stars are endowed with soul life. I want to renew this knowledge.

"The planets in the vicinity of your earth are keepers of divine power. Their nucleus is visible, but they have a cover, which you cannot see, on which the angelic realms of power are located. All stars are bound to one another by mysterious currents; a web of rays, harbouring time and eternity, flows around them.

"The stars bring you both favourable and unfavourable conditions. Guided by divine spirits, they shine upon you from the beginning to the end of life. They have raised generation upon generation; they have broken down the blockades of an idle nature and caused the stream of life to flow; they have ignited the glow of souls to become the fire of temperaments and they have stood guard over the fate of nations. They have elevated and destroyed, overthrown and built up, punished and rewarded, withdrawn and endowed, blessed and pardoned and thus caused the human souls to develop over the millenia.

"Stars—gods—angels: the all-providing life force of the one most glorious spirit whom we call God.

"God. His feeling, his will, his love influence you through the stars' miraculous inter-relations. Fanned out in the angels' activities, he is reflected like the sparkle of the sun on the ocean waves. And the imperfections of the earth fade to nothing in the face of the eternity of his supremely perfect creation of spirit existence.

"Mankind has long known that there is a connection between the cosmos and human fate. However, it is not the stars, suns and planets but the great, divine spirits who influence you from there. They are powers who serve God. In figure and countenance they resemble the gods of antiquity. Past cultures were able to recognise some of them, but they could not understand the important, holy causal relations. God has no gods next to him. All divine spirits are subordinate to him.

"When you look up to the canopy of stars, you should know that on all sides God's sons and daughters look down on you. They are those angels of fate whom we also call star-gods, because they fulfill particular tasks. Among them are judges and deputies of law. You know from the Psalms that even in ancient times the judges were called 'gods'.*

"The gods of history, whose names varied, were exalted spirits who were positioned in the currents of the stars that God guided. Human errors and misunderstandings, which arose from the misinterpretation of extrasensory perceptions and developed into cruel animal sacrifices† and immoral cults, induced God to extinguish completely the belief in gods.

"But over the millenia the glory of the angels aspires towards the high and holy goal of mature mankind.

"Happiness and unhappiness, joy and sorrow, pain and pleasure are assigned to you people of this earth according to the measure and

---

*Psalm 82: "God standeth in the congregation of the mighty; he judgeth among the gods."

†God's rejection of animal sacrifices is also mentioned in the Psalms:

50: "The mighty God, even the Lord, hath spoken and called the earth from the rising of the sun unto the going down thereof."

50/9: "I will take no bullock out of thy house, nor he-goats out of thy folds."

50/10: "For every beast of the forest is mine, and the cattle upon a thousand hills."

50/13: "Will I eat the flesh of bulls, or drink the blood of goats?"

50/14: "Offer unto God thanksgiving; and pay thy vows unto the most high."

design of the eternal governors of fate.

"In the course of these reports you will get to know some of these sublime spirits of heaven who execute the holy will of the Creator.

"You assume you are dealing with the radiant energy of stars when you study your horoscopes. Hear therefore the following explanation: The mighty angels of the stars are God's authorised servants. They fulfil his commands and his spirit permeates them. Although their actions are neither lenient nor indulgent, they are just and fair in a measure that stands above the earthly course of life and they bear witness to his love for you—a love that shines out into eternity.

"If you go through this life without burdening yourselves with heavy sins, you have the possibility of gaining the goodwill and the affection of the angels of fate. You may talk to them and ask help from those who have expressed the desire to make themselves known; who no longer wish to remain in the secrecy of the universe of stars.

"Only some of them comply with the prayers of human beings and have turned to God with the request to be introduced to you. Only some of them—the others do not wish it. Those, however, who do wish to be addressed by you in prayer, desire personal contact with you in the future, in order to be able to influence your purification more strongly. For your souls, minds and hearts are to be purified. And you must take advantage of the strong power of prayer.

"Now let me explain to you how you should pray. First address yourselves to God the Lord, the Creator of all life. Send him rays of love from your hearts and then ask to be heard by those angels to whom you wish to turn at this particular moment. The secret of fortification lies in this kind of prayer.

"Give the star-gods above you the power to change a certain condition in your fate through the current of spiritual contact with them. I have chosen to reveal the following secret to you: There is no spirit being in heaven who would not listen to a human request. A request that is spoken from the depth of the soul always penetrates into the hearts of the angels, always moves them. They then strive to comply with the request, so that it can be granted within the pattern of fate assigned to you and they deliberate your prayers within the circle of God's authorised servants.

"The star current influencing you at the time can be altered. The stars governing your destiny are not rigid; they can be swayed. If a divine ordinance seems to be too severe to you, then there are possibilities of relief through your souls' strong bond with God. Even the most difficult fate in life can be alleviated through the strengthening of your souls.

"Thrive, my people, for the God of the star world, for the God of love, as the most beautiful, most magnificent flower garden!

"And as the flowers unfold towards the sun, so turn your hearts to the light of the Holy Spirit. Open yourselves to the glory of heaven, you souls of immortality!"

FIGHTING SICKNESS WITH THE ASSISTANCE OF SPIRITUAL HELPERS—SIXTUS

"THE first of the heavenly spirit beings I want to introduce to you is a powerful and—for all of you—a very important star-ruler. As an angel of fate he is on that frequency of radiation that beams down on you from the constellation of Pisces. His name is Sixtus.

"He is a strict son of God who commands obedience. His appearance is magnificent, in accordance with the Creator's desire for beauty. His countenance is of such noble expression that his arrival at the circle of gods causes a stir of excitement. Do not imagine the star-gods to be like the angels in your picture books. The angels of fate resemble the gods as portrayed by the ancient Greeks, but even these give only a poor indication of the sublime beauty of the sons and daughters of God. A diffused radiance is spread over them and they all reflect his majesty.

"So imagine Sixtus to be of a very masculine appearance with a bearing of grandeur. His eyes, which in happy moments shine with a wonderful warmth, are over-shadowed by bushy brows. His mouth, in contrast to the warm expression in his eyes, hints at severity. But when Sixtus flares up in a rage, his eyes emit sparks and no one responsible for his anger can escape.

"Sixtus is the leading physician in the world beyond. We have no diseases, no germs, no viruses, but we do have doctors. On the one hand, they work as soul attendants in the spheres of stars, in fields of duty which I cannot explain to you here. On the other hand they are indispensable for the earth.

"There is a certain, all-pervading ministration of spirit powers that is unknown to you. In this way your physicians often work under the thought influence of these spirit helpers. Through suggestions whispered into the brains of their charges they implant enlightening ideas. They influence them in a manner similar to that of guardian angels, whose work they complement. These call upon them whenever necessary.

"However, if earthly physicians are impure in their soul substance, if they are inferior characters and allow themselves to be guided by base instincts, if they are godless, emotionally cold and place their own earthly happiness above the evaluation of the need and suffering of their patients, their senses are closed to divine inspiration. As I have already said: only an open vessel can be filled.

"Now, it is not only to doctors that these helpers are assigned. All of you can ask for spiritual healing. It complements earthly medical treatment.

"There are sects who decline medical intervention, because they maintain that all suffering is given by God and has to be accepted. These people are mistaken. God has given man a mind and has developed his scientific knowledge. It can therefore never be God's wish that the human mind lies fallow. It is his aspiration to advance the human soul to the highest degree of maturity. People who refuse an operation for themselves or their children, when this is the only way to save a life, deprive God of the maturation of a soul.

"One should only resign oneself to one's fate when all earthly and spiritual means of healing fail. Only then comes the surrender to inevitable destiny.

"When you people are in poor health, go to your doctors as usual. When you have received medical treatment, call at the same time upon the healing powers of heaven. On millions of occasions we find that people who fall sick resign themselves to their fate in a kind of paralysing submission. They have drifted so far away from faith, that it does not even occur to them to pray. Excluded from the circle of the healthy, they give themselves sleepless nights through completely unnecessary fears and worries.

"Those who suffer from cancer or other serious diseases are in a state of utmost despair. They behave like drowning castaways who do not even open their eyes to search the horizon for possibilities of rescue. The doctor's diagnosis hits them like a hammer blow and they stand aghast in the face of such horror.

"All in all, the measures taken to heal cancer, this disorder of the tissue, are the right ones. The degenerate tissue has to be removed. Even then, the fear of a new outbreak of the disease remains. However, this fear promotes the disease. Hear now how you must behave in such cases:

"In the domain of stars a powerful physician is at your disposal. Now when you lie on your sickbed, do not capitulate to fear. Enlist the help of the stars, which will be granted to you with the greatest love if you follow my instructions.

"Never yield to the idea that a sickness is incurable! The severest diseases can be healed, if not by earthly medicine, then by a combination of earthly and divine spiritual healing.

"If a doctor gives up a case as hopeless, his bond with God is not sufficiently strong. I am not talking here about people who are dying, but about patients who still have the spirit of life and vigour. The soul body inside you cannot be affected by earthly sicknesses and injuries. It remains healthy within the sick physical body.

"When Sixtus, or a spirit doctor sent by him, treats you, he beams the organ in your soul body which is sick in your physical body. Through increased radiant energy to the soul organ or to entire sections of the body that are endangered, your weakened body is built up. The cells are strengthened anew, the circulation is stimulated, the forces of resistance are considerably intensified and a process of purification takes place.

"This is the secret of my miraculous healing which I effected as God's son of man on earth. I prayed to be given the greatest healing powers of the Holy Spirit. My prayer was heard and granted.

"In this age man has detached himself from God and deprived himself of the most wonderful currents of help which the cosmos is ready to offer. You are in a phase of development that leads to maturity through a serious crisis. The nations of the world are still caught up in a strong urge to fight one another. They will still severely injure one another. But this time is coming to an end. Then a new age will dawn in which the soul's reliance on God will enable mankind to advance.

"The preparation for the era of man's reliance on God is beginning now. Each one of you must cast off your lethargy and move towards this sublime goal! In each one of you is an antenna which is able to receive God's currents. Start to use it again. Even if the relations between the super powers are still in a state of turmoil, even if there is fighting in various parts of the world, everyone should still be aware of his holy commitment to God. This commitment is what gives him personally the greatest help in life."

THE STAR VENUS

"ALEMEILA is the name of the angelic daughter of God who was once known as Aphrodite. She was given many other names: Kypris, Paphia, Amathusia and Idalia. Her star is shining Venus. As love unites two sexes, God has assigned the star of love to a pair of angels. Alemelia lives in eternal union with her husband, Amerides.

"God's love is incomprehensible to you humans. It shines down on you in a myriad currents.

"Just as you may turn to Sixtus with every health problem, you may now ask Alemeila and Amerides for help if you have problems in love or marriage. Sometimes the expression of a thought is blocked by feelings of shame and keeps you from addressing Mary in prayer. Her holy love is of sublime purity and above all human sensual feelings. But you may now approach the noble lovers of heaven without any inhibitions. They understand every anxiety, every request and every wish that has to do with the sexual emotions of love. But they demand the very highest degree of decency of character and purity of heart and soul as a pre-requisite for hearing and granting your prayers.

"Alemeila is a vision of God. She has become the living image of the tenderness of his heart. She emanates the eternal magic of feminine beauty and nobility. She is the most auspicious fulfillment of divine desire for grace and tender sensitivity. Her wonderful thoughts delight the angels of heaven and the gestures of humility with which she pays respect to the Father are of indescribable beauty. Of indescribable beauty too is her face and her whole figure. To the blessed she is like a fairy princess. The magic she radiates is the happy shine of love—a love that embraces both the most intense spiritual emotion and the tender, sweet giving and taking of sensual feeling.

"In past ages Amerides was known as Hephaistos, the husband of Aphrodite. But through faulty recognition man endowed him with incorrect traits. The physically disabled Hephaistos does not exist.

"Amerides is as handsome as the bright morning. His love for

Alemeila is most holy. His radiance streams through the mysterious, tender depths of her being. With his sunny and cheerfully convincing manner he is the picture of divine joy of life, but he also embodies a deep seriousness and the most angelic tenderness of feeling. He is tall and slender and unusually agile because, with his love of perfect beauty, he has developed his body to the ultimate expressiveness of movement. This is why he commands the Muse of dancing, as you call it. Know that the art of dancing is one of God's many gifts to mankind.

"Angels were the gods and Muses of past cultures, for God has always sent his protecting, enlightening spirit powers down to earth.

"Together with Alemeila, Amerides belongs to the great spirit beings of heaven who influence man's sense of beauty, love, art and culture. The heart's most tender emotions are guided by the radiance from the spirit sphere of Venus; but it also ignites the fire of passion.

"Whenever love's exalted emotions in man are disturbed by base thoughts arising from the obscure depths of the soul; whenever those spell-bound by the mysterious charms of love contemplate evil; whenever odious phantoms of passion like jealousy and hate are present; whenever a soul wades through the swamp of sensual decay; whenever people with abnormal sexual urges—people who are shameless and far from God—seek to drown their passions in perversions, the star-couple turns away. And the sense of shame of the other angels is also offended.

"People who do not hold sacred the bounds of nature and violate animals or children, or yield to sadism, prove the inferiority of their souls. For man's will can stave off the body's urges by turning his soul to God. And the sickness of such inclinations can be healed by prayer.

"The laws of nature are born out of God's spirit. There is order in the arrangement of all life—keep it sacred! Strive for order in the holy possession of both life and love, you who are God's hope for the future. Spiritual and bodily purity should always be a matter of course and with God's love the angels will make you gifts of selected treasures."

THE STAR MARS

"ERVINIUS is the name of the angelic son of God who rules Mars, the planet close to earth. It is his task to beam strength to man. He draws this strength from God and channels it into individual fates, that is, to individuals.

"His appearance is the picture of strength. Powerful and majestic, he takes his place in the governing body of the gods. He belongs to the council of the great powers who govern time and destiny's hour. He is not a god of war, not a destroyer, but a conqueror of all weaknesses.

"Courage and strength of heart are the gifts of Ervinius and calmness and composure in the storm of life. The ray he directs into your hearts offers self-confidence and assurance. So he assists those whom God calls to power. The leaders of the earth who are under his guidance stand before God in magnanimity and righteousness. He tolerates nothing false. Nothing base can develop under his exalted influence. Whoever manages to gain the support of this son of the Father of all the mighty star-ruling powers will never be endangered by hatred, ill-will and the filth of inferior souls. He stands far above all that is evil in human nature, secure in the knowledge that he is on the right path. I do not shun these mighty rulers of the earth, oh my people.* They are the hope and the wealth of my heart. The wealth I would now like to increase in this world.

"Therefore, I tell you: call upon the powers of heaven through ardent prayers which you must send into God's soul. God's triune majesty is above your stars. In the name of the Father, the Son and the Holy Spirit ask for the inflow from the powers and you will receive it.

"Mars, as you may also call Ervinius, is hallowed in the spirit of God, like all the rulers of powers and thrones of heaven. Mars overcomes every weakness in your hearts; he overcomes discontent and hopelessness; he gives life force and energy. But he is not only well-disposed towards those in power. Oh no, he can free even the weakest from their lethargy and to everybody who asks for help he shows equal affection."

THE STAR MERCURY

"MERCURIUS has been known to man since time immemorial. In the starry sky he stands above the historical concept of Hermes. From astrological experience you know of the power of the energy that

*See chapter "A Warning to Everyone".

radiates from the sun-bound planet Mercury. It is the vocation of the son of God who guides it to smooth people's professional way through life. His influence on your mind stimulates your enjoyment of work, of professional advancement and of striving for success. He wakens in you feelings of self-confidence and, through impulses of initiative, he conquers indifference, laziness and timidity. He inspires and gives ideas. His secret is the arrangement of contacts between people. He paves the way for relations that are important for people's life work, directs you into good professional careers and draws together human fates whose paths indicate a common goal according to divine wishes. In this way he operates as a lively, versatile, slender and youthful star-god, who watches over your business and professional relations.

"The planet itself is only the location for the measurements and computer-like calculations conducted under the command of this son of God whom you may call Mercury. His angelic name is Deiamos. Deiamos and Hermes are not identical. Deiamos stands above Hermes. So it is that from the partial knowledge of the sublime angels of fate, man moulded the images and natures of his gods.

"Mercury is now willing to receive your requests and to help you with your professional worries and problems through benefits beamed from his star, even if the total constellation is not a favourable one. He has excellent, friendly relations with all divine powers and forces. In order to help you, he needs your prayers to God, whose holy current of love he taps, just as do all the other administrators of the stars. At the will of almighty God he commands the hour and the day, and to all aspiring souls he is an amiable, helpful, magnificent friend.*

COSMIC RAYS

"THE gods who guide the stars are judges; they are builders of souls through the disposition of fate and they are both punishing and rewarding executives of God. They all love mankind deeply. They all harbour the love of the Father, whom they serve. When they punish, they do so with a heavy heart. Whenever the worth of a soul develops under their eyes, they all rejoice.

---

*Jesus has not yet given me a message about Jupiter. But Osario, an angel of fate from the northern heavens, gave me information about him. (See page 147.)

"They are eternally marked by their gender. Wherever masculine force is at work, there must be feminine feeling as well. So the hosts of angels are divided into masculine and feminine heirs of the most holy prime spirit, the cosmic One who made himself a gift by achieving God: the Holy Spirit—eternal cause, eternal source of all that exists; the original power of omnipotence in which everything that was to be divided, was united. The angels are the heirs of this One in whom God exists.

"When the heavens shine for you at night, go down on your knees, for you are looking into the countenance of the Eternal One. When you rise again, you are consecrated. Heaven and its wonderful power looks down upon you. Beholding the stars, you behold the beginning of eternal bliss. God's glory lies spread out before you and so does God's love. And God's feeling is spread out across the immeasurable space above you in which the works of the most sublime spirit beings are woven into the pattern of the stars, according to the most holy designs.

"This pattern of revolving stars, established out of the horror of chaos, is the work of God. In the universal storm of development, by the immense might of his will, by the power of his thought, by the magic force of his word, he enforced the evolutionary maturation from matter and spheric elements to the unified nature of the one mighty cosmos. This surpasses in size and composition everything that human beings can imagine; even angels are moved by its immensity.

"Omnipotence lies in God's word. 'In the beginning was the word,' an enlightened person wrote you. Hear now that there is magic power in your words too. But only dare to use this magic power for good purposes. For God reserves a terrible punishment for those who try to obtain power through evil thoughts!

"I want to make you the gift of the knowledge of the most holy miracles. There are forces in the stars that you can take advantage of. If you stir up these powers through strong thoughts, through intense currents emitted from the mind, you force them to listen to you and to help you; for in all of them is God's love for his human beings which you, the Father's children who have gone astray, should recognise again.

"The stars are bound together through mysterious currents and equipped with the most wonderful frequency-receiving stations. Imagine these as supremely sophisticated installations, which can be read by the angels. Automatic records are collected, observed, evaluated, co-ordinated and processed at the highest level. In this way, great, eternal star marvels are at the disposal of the builders of souls up there, and with their help they can act with absolute justice—justice not confined to one earthly life, but embracing all the reincarnations. It is a justice also in the Christian sense, in the examination of the values of souls, as well as in the detached sense of spirit elevation or degradation of people who have been tested and have made their way through one or several lives."

POOR SOULS

"SOULS are not always to be redeemed from the earth-bound after-life state in which they need purification. Very much evil, which remains for generations, adheres to some people. When souls are purified and return over and over again to a new life and fail repeatedly, then the observing powers of justice who watch over them have a way to invigorate and improve the substance of their souls. They bind such souls to the earth after death. Therefore, the grievous failures who are unable to rise above sin; who are unable to improve the value of their souls in one incarnation after the other; who continually show the same aberrations, continually practise the same evil and purposely defy the divine commandments of the Christian doctrine, or whatever religion they belong to—these people who repeatedly damage the holy gift of a pure soul must suffer the heavy penance of being bound to the earth.

"In a state of utmost yearning for redemption, they wander through its spheric orbit. They are the poor souls for whom you so often pray so compassionately. They are really very much in need of your prayers for, since they are outcasts, nobody hears their prayers. No one from the angelic host pays attention to them. Deeply unhappy, they remain far from the glory and blessing of God. If you pray for such souls, your prayers will be heard if your hearts are pure and those unhappy wanderers on whom the radiance of your love will shine in accordance with the holy laws of love, are pardoned. Thoughts of love also serve as a preparation for redemption.

"If it seems likely to you that one of your relatives, friends or acquaintances might be in need of redemption, then pray for him and think of him with feelings of love, although you were aware of his sins. In this way you achieve an earlier pardon for him.

"It is certain that every soul will be pardoned one day, but those who are unredeemed long most intensely for your prayers."

THE TURNING-POINT OF TIME

THE present constellation of the stars indicates the same significant mission as it did at the time of my birth. It indicates a great turning point in time. The sky resembles a stage on which the scenery is being changed.*

"Lift yourselves up my people, from your earth-bound thinking. Recognise eternity. Call a halt to resigned reasoning. Release yourselves from pent-up fears and give free reign, you who are bound to God, to the currents of the heart. The way to salvation is open to you and you shall all be blessed."

BLESSED ARE . . .

"BLESSED are those who reciprocate the love of God's son while they are still on earth, for the Holy Spirit endows them with the greatest soul maturity.

"Blessed are those who love, for they live in God's soul.

"Blessed are those who do not bury the treasure of sacred hope, for they are constructing the new age.

"Blessed are those who shed tears for the suffering on earth, for their tears moisten the hand of God and God's hand is raised to alleviate the suffering.

"Blessed are those who have passed the exacting tests of the stars for they will be transformed like butterflies which, freed from their dark cocoons, rise to flight in sunny gardens.

"Blessed are the tender souls for, far from the bustling world, they behold God in every creature, in everything that blooms on earth and their rising thanks fill his heart with joy.

"Blessed are those who listen within, for they hear the angel's voice.

"Blessed are those who behave like thorns in order to protect God's

---

*Message received on January 14, 1981. Astronomically it was a significant day. It was the first meeting of Jupiter and Saturn.

roses. They fight for the holy possession of faith, they preserve the pure heritage of religion for the children. They plough God's fields and sow his love repeatedly among the people. They are blessed, these keepers of faith, for God places their gifts high on the table of enrichment, where they shine in the light of his gratitude.

"Blessed, oh blessed are all those who experience God's gratitude; the gratitude of eternity for the gift of the soul who, while living on earth, has understood his love."

SHADOW AND LIGHT

"SHADOWS are spread across today's earth. This planet's realm of creation is in twilight, but in the gloom we can see treasures shine like diamonds and pearls. It is the will of God that these are salvaged.

"There are multitudes who live far from God as opposed to those who are divinely enlightened. The latter must recognise and overcome the imperfections of their brothers and sisters.

"Happiness on earth is limited and the suffering of life cannot always be avoided. Extreme suffering is experienced by tender souls who believe their beloved ones to be dying. So they believe, but death is only transformation. The suffering is most severe when the life of a beloved child leaves its earthly body.

"It is one of the most difficult trials on earth to bear such suffering without rebelling against God in heart-felt anguish. The constant prayer of love is: protect and guard the ones I love.

"It is not God's hand that causes you sorrow. Severe disturbances in the nature of the body are the cause of many a sickness and many an early death.

"God has forced life to obey the laws of nature. His unshakeable will has achieved the eternal life of the soul, which has only been made possible through the construction of the earthly body. His love endures beyond the temporal limitations of your earthly existence. Never surrender in despair to bitterness against God!

"God is supreme love! And the glory of his grace also embraces your profoundest grief."

GUARDIAN ANGELS

"ANGELS filled with happiness are contributing to the construction of a new age. They give those who call them life's happiness in the measure of their grace; they bless those, who dedicate themselves to the Creator, with treasures, which they pluck from the currents of the stars. Everyone who kept his heart pure has the angel in his close vicinity; an angel who is familiar with his being, with his feelings, thinking, fears, with his life's activity on earth, and who accompanies him in deepest love.

"But even he who sinned and failed is not deserted by his angel if he feels shame and remorse. And if he invokes the angel, who has loved him since his first hour, who knows him with all his weaknesses, all his mistaken thoughts, which led him astray to foolish behaviour or evil deeds, then filled with love, he will guide him from his confused life on to the right path. Nobody on this earth is lonely!

"A strong cord links every human being to the guardian angel assigned to him by God. Your future endeavour must be to strengthen this. Through mental conversation you bind your angel to you and it is his greatest joy to be in the presence of his beloved child—for all of you are children!

"Do not be timid about making demands on your angelic companion. His proximity gives you great strength. If you forget him, he moves to a higher sphere. Even there he is linked to you and keeps an eye on you, but you are much happier when he remains close to you.

"There is an angel to look after every person. Bear in mind that if you are timid about calling your angel, you cast a gloom over his life's happiness. Also remember that the earth's living space is divided into the region of heavy matter and that of spiritual existence. It is in the latter that the angels live, surrounded by beauty.

"The number of men and angels may seem incredibly high to you, but in God's sight it is very small. With effortless ease the sublime spirit beings oversee the existence of several billion earthly souls. Completely different numbers fill the cosmos. God governs worlds which multiply as the universe expands. There is infinite space that still needs to be populated with life of spirit and soul.

"Contrary to incarnate life, soul life is sustained by the rays of God.

Therefore, it cannot be dissolved, but remains in eternity.

"Number and space are infinite in God's universe. Infinite in that they are unlimited. The universe is expanding; it is expanding into eternity until one day it will dissolve into light and glory, just as man detaches himself from flesh and blood when he rises into the light of God.

"The holy work of the Deity is the preservation of cosmic life with the ultimate goal of transformation into light. Man serves the sublime purpose of the spiritualisation of the cosmic being. He is to live in the spiritual centre of the universe in order to fulfil an infinite variety of tasks.

"The angels fulfil vital tasks; but God also assigns vital tasks to those people of spirit life-form whose souls have matured to perfection.

"Man's eternal bliss is the consequence of the maturation, the highest evolution of human soul-value that leads to the blessed vision of the Deity, to the unity of God and the enlightened man in the Holy Spirit, in the utmost bliss of love.

"Unity with God is only possible in the feeling of deepest humility —a humility that thrives in the reflection of God's glory.

"All wanderers through the spheres of the Holy Spirit strive towards this supreme goal. They attain it in the happiness of turning to the light, in the happiness of commitment to the angels, in the happiness of devotion to great tasks and in the happiness of the genuine joy of life which, permeated by the holy surges of divine love, all souls feel."

SUBLIMITY OF THE SOUL

"ONLY very few people achieve a sublime soul on earth. Nobody achieves the absolute purity of heart reflected in completely flawless and sinless conduct. You are all weak and egoistical. The holiest man too has moments of weakness and even when he has reached the highest level of human greatness, he must constantly pray for enlightenment in order not to revert to the shadows of the earth from which he has withdrawn. If God's mercy, the forgiveness of sins and the compassion of love did not exist, heaven would be empty and would wait thousands of years for human souls.

"Because of the sacrifice of the love of his son, God decided to free mankind from the ties of reincarnation and grant forgiveness to the sinners and those who had stumbled if the essence of their souls remained pure and healthy. The purity of the essence of the soul must be preserved, for a deeply corrupt man falls from the tree of life like a rotten fruit.

"There are people in the sphere of punishment who can be considered irretrievably lost; people who, despite every experience of suffering, do not repent. No one suffers a degree of agony in the so-called 'hell' in excess of what he himself has callously inflicted upon other living beings while on earth. But even these people, hopelessly hardened in sin, will be led back to a new beginning in life after they have suffered their punishment.

"Therefore, eternal damnation means that the worst sinners will never behold God as they are, but they will look upon the light of the earth again and here they have the opportunity to change.

"What must you believers do now, in order to obtain the purity of heart and soul desired by God?

"You have learned that 'he who knows his heart to be pure, has his guardian angel next to him'. Now you examine yourselves and you find many a blemish that you have been able to live with very comfortably. When you realise that you are sinful and long for the angel, listen to the voice of conscience and examine in how far the evil you are doing is of vital importance to you. Confession, which the members of the Catholic church make, is of great value if it is carried out in honest repentance and effects a change in the way of life. However, repeated begging for forgiveness when moral conduct is unworthy offends the angels' feelings.

"When you receive a priest's absolution, bear in mind that he cannot look into the depths of your soul; but your angel can and your most secret thoughts do not escape him.

"At the moment of birth every soul is white and filled with glory, for it comes from the kingdom of God. The souls of those who have stumbled and have been cleansed are just as pure as the souls of the saints who volunteered for reincarnation in order to instruct and teach the people of this earth. Souls who are burdened by an earlier, mis-spent life bear its guilt in their karma, which is only visible to the angels. This means they are pure in their new life and only in the book of God is a record kept of their guilt, whose burden forced them back to earth.

"If you overcome the selfishness within you and rise from the depths of craving for pleasure at all costs, the angels will protect and help you.

"Happiness on earth is not denied to you; you may aspire to it, but you will never mature here through pleasure alone. Pleasure shall only be compensation and relaxation.

"You have only received this life on earth in order to prepare yourselves for God's sublime and wonderful world. Everybody will mature here until God considers he is worthy to set foot on the hallowed ground of his sacred spheres; those sacred spheres in which no evil can exist.

"God's kingdom has been opened for you, but you may only enter it in purity."

SPHERES OF PURIFICATION

"HEAVENLY life never dies, but it changes. All of you who dwell on earth must acquire a mature soul. The soul's value or lack thereof determines into which of the heavenly spheres you are accepted after earthly death.

"The high judges tend to re-unite you according to your generation and earthly associations. They tend to do this, but they are able to do so for only part of mankind. People whose basic soul values are good and noble will live in the sphere of pure light, which they may enter immediately after their purification. By spheres I mean the planets of light whose zoning is arranged according to the harmonic laws of the cosmos. We have planets of purification where people experience soul purging under severe conditions, where they suffer punishment and are heavily burdened by their own mistakes and the sins they committed on earth against the better judgement of their conscience.

"There are realms of imperfect hearts and those of uncontrolled desires. We have sites where those afflicted by intellectual pride meet, where those filled with hatred are at the mercy of one another, where misers keep misers company, where members of secret societies—like their earthly victims—fall prey to the lawless deeds of their congregations.

"We have stars where the countless cheats and liars of this earth dwell closely together in sad disgrace and other stars for those who trespassed against the laws of decency and modesty because of greed for money gained from vice. The severest punishment for sinners is that they are exposed to themselves. To themselves and their equals. Amends are made for matrimonial perfidies by the endurance of exactly the same tricks as were used before. However, the couples are separated. Powerlessly, evil is exposed to evil. The punishment is to suffer the baseness of one's own soul.

"We have realms where the vilest vermin conceived by the human brain and—contrary to the laws of divine harmony—called 'art' has taken shape. In these zones, where all that is natural is deformed and every sense of beauty is disregarded, must live those who created such monstrosities, thereby enriching themselves while ignoring the divine law, which was present and tangible even in them.

"People impose the heaviest burdens on themselves if they only regard earthly life as valuable and important; earthly life and its enjoyment.

"The zones of purification can only be left when the individual, deeply nauseated by himself and his like, implores cleansing and rescue. Then great, strong spirit beings come from the ranks of noble souls and beam in love. They bring brightness, and strengthen and point the penitent to a higher sphere where there is light and happiness awaits him.

"Those unfortunate people who on earth paved the way for the world of shadows—the so-called 'hell'—suffer there exactly the measure of anguish and pain they caused others while living on earth. In some cases that particularly provoke the judges, the degree of punishment is significantly increased, up to a hundred-fold and more times the pain that was inflicted. This is the case in the murder of children. The killing of a child and cruelty to helpless victims are the most serious crimes against God and are severely atoned for. Murder, committed arbitrarily and in full possession of mental health, calls for the severest punishment.

"Brutalities of the heart, expressed through the torture of animals, through cruel treatment of God's creatures by way of exploitation, extermination, utilisation with a view to financial gain, unnatural caging, agonising transportation or inhuman experiments conducted without anaesthetics are punished on an isolated planet. There the sinners against nature are presented with a phantom image of every single animal they have mistreated and they have to suffer the agonies of each one of them.

"Depraved and evil people—those who scorn God, who hate God

and are felons against the laws of love—have no access to the soul's path of salvation for all eternity. They can never ascend to a higher sphere, even after they have suffered all punishments. They can only hope for the mercy of reincarnation, nothing else and this only if they plead in deepest remorse for God's grace.

SALVATION

"I AM he who prepares the salvation of all souls. The wealth I grant you is love and life, humility and sublimity, modesty and generosity, gentleness and strictness. For I grant you the wealth of power over time, the wealth of the heart's nobility, the wealth of hope that knows its fulfilment in the changing of times.

"The number that binds you to hour and day, to heaviness and blood, to shadow and light, space and confinement, to substance and solidity—this number will be changed.

"Power is wealth. Power is strength. Power is security and tranquillity. Power is nothing if these values can turn to dust and ashes. And all violence is destined to go this way.

"Nothing endures in the realm of matter, but the power of the soul is holy; holy too, the power that flows from God's heart. It alone can guide you to the path of salvation. This power forces all weapons that rise against it into dust, breaks the barriers of all borders, grows and thrives under the protection of the Lord of the world of stars.

"Achieve the power of the stars, my people, the power of the stars! And then heaven will grant you celestial bliss while you are still on earth."

THE SOUL'S PATH TO SALVATION

"IN THE kingdom of the Holy Trinity great realms of stars have been founded; spirit realms of stars to which people are assigned. These stars whose nuclei consist of heavy matter—by this I mean atoms with which you are familiar—are kingdoms of magnificence. The inhabitants of these regions behold the son of God on many important festive days of the year, although they are far from being accepted into the spheres of the highest purity.

"As most people live there for a very long time—for centuries by earthly standards and even longer if necessary—this life in the spheres shall be described to you.

"There live your loved ones who have departed from you. They are happy and cheerful people whose hearts are filled with God's radiance. They have differing degrees of maturity, but are grouped together, not according to the level of maturity, but according to their relations on earth. The angels who assign them their places in this realm of life take into account ties of family and friendship, but not the degree of maturity of the soul.

"So the conditions of life are similar to those on earth. The spheres of soul maturation are distributed among several stars which circle around a sun according to the laws of the cosmos. The day begins for the people up there as it does here, with a sunrise.

"I said as a man 'In my Father's house are many mansions.' Now let me describe to you the mansions in the world of stars where gifts of God await you such as you cannot imagine.

"For you, 'heaven' begins with your rise from the zones of purification. Heaven—the world of joy, of redemption from all the distress, from all the suffering and all earthly pain.

"Oh understand, you unbelievers: The son of God has opened the gates to this world for you. Understand too, you believers of the powerful non-Christian world religions, that these gates would remain closed to you if, above all limited human understanding, above all life on this earth would not be the mighty heart of love of the one whom you do not recognise as God!

"You also, my faithful ones of Christianity, understand this: my love fills the whole earth! My love enters into every noble human soul, into every innocent creature. My love stands as high above all human imaginative faculties as the sun stands above all life on this earth.

"The Messiah you have attached yourselves to as Christians is more than just the God of your doctrines. He is the highest spirit in the cosmos, next to God the Father and the Holy Spirit. His sublime love is above all that words of old scriptures can convey to you.

"I, the Lord of the worlds, have prepared the path of salvation for the souls.

"Do you believe that the most free and supreme spirit of the universe, the son of God, who created all men, would be restrained in his loving?

"Rise above the confines of your religion. Open yourselves to the light of knowledge, the knowledge of my immeasurable, world-wide and world-unifying love. Every one of you is born into this love and has indiscriminate rights to God's heaven.

The sole right to supreme happiness in those shining realms of God is not reserved for my Catholic Christianity, as they sometimes think. I gave the Father blood and tears, so that he would redeem *all* mankind and free them from these strong ties to the earth.

"When the blessed, whose birth and education enabled them to follow my teachings, behold heaven, they will find innumerable people there who were not bound to the Church, either because of fate or because of their own free will. Nevertheless, they lived their lives closely attached to God's heart and are now blessed, with his grace and love.

"It is the wealth of the heart that leads into these spheres. The wealth that everybody can achieve on this earth.

"Disseminated in all human hearts is goodness, is love, is the holy seed that bears God's hope. Disseminated so that it may develop and prepare the fruit which, after flowering in this earthly life, is presented like a harvest offering on the holy altar of the Deity to increase the colourful multitude of gifts. For your pure heart is a gift to the Father. The supreme heart of love rejoices at such maturity achieved from the strength of the tender seed.

"Each one of you is presented with such a gift when your earthly life's path begins.

"Even in the greatest misery, God's seeds blossom. Strong and indestructible, they blossom and bear fruit.

"Love is the name of the ground that enables God's seed to grow. Only love, for man's mind and intellect are earthly attributes, not distributed in equal measure.

"Mind and intellect are the individual's inheritance, predominantly biologically imprinted, like the shape of the body and the features of the face, as well as distinctive characteristics which are preserved across the centuries.

"The mind can be damaged by disturbances of the overall physical condition. It can be handicapped from birth in its development. Therefore, those who feel mentally superior to others, be happy, but without pride, for on the scales of the highest judges the side which contains life's values will sink, not because of the weight of mental achievements but because of the vibrations of love which streamed forth from your hearts throughout your life.

"Where the mind, highly developed through diligence and aspiration, unites with love's holy force, the happiest fulfilment of a person's life is achieved. Even if the outer radiance of life on earth is missing on account of life's hardships, the angels perceive glory and light in the inner heart and soul.

"The soul's path to salvation is open to everybody on earth. Heaven awaits you. Inviolable, eternal laws bind God's world. Without these laws everything would dissolve into chaos. The universe is a vast government system.

"The living space of the part of the cosmos that can be seen from the earth is the head of the cosmic figure. Here glow the suns of divine will-power. Here the greatest miracle of God's creation originated: the spheric glow of life transcending the ordered system of planets and suns of heavy matter. It is a glow of the higher realm of stars.

"Matter is vibration. The light matter in the world beyond consists of waves of vibration with a weaker concentration—therefore, with larger, wider wave-lengths than earthly matter. The hard, heavy matter of your living space is created by the closeness of the waves, which tautens the vibrations.

"In the zone of light, in the kingdom of God, vibrations of rich diversity have spread out just like sound waves. Thus, in the universe, elements of life, which had evolved on planets orbiting around their suns, came into existence. From these God moulded his creation. A host of spirits operates everywhere according to God's will and is actively concerned with order and development.

"However, man's intellect is not powerful enough to understand the world of stars in its boundless magnitude. Man's mind cannot conceive the eternal.

"Therefore, from numerical infinity and a wealth of creation, return to your earth from which holy, spiritual currents flow to the living space of the Godhead. These rays are produced by the rays of consciousness of human minds.

"The mind of man has a strong radiation. Situated in the human forehead and protected by the cerebral cortex is the most sensitive transmitting device. It is a 'device' in terms of its technical characteristics, for according to the physical laws of God, you do not only consist of body and soul, but also of an energy current which ignites your mind. This current is charged by divine impulses. Through specific reactions of the soul, reflexes are formed which act on the bio-recorder in your brain, transforming the emotional vibrations of the soul into radio-waves. Guided by large currents, these flow directly to the Godhead. Immense powers have been implanted into nature.

"Godhead means: the one God who represents the utmost peak of all spiritual life. He is the God whose son I am and whose primal force is the Holy Spirit. The Godhead therefore is the Trinity, it also represents a power of perception superior to anything that man can imagine. All of you are recorded, all the vibrations of your soul are recorded and so are all your thoughts, for you have been created solely for eternal life. Otherwise, for those few years given to you here, your life on earth would be completely meaningless.

"These recordings are made in hemispheres of observation which God erected on stars of light matter. Created through energies of the divine spirit, they are the greatest technical wonders.

"All life on earth glides through the mortal frame; through flesh and blood and biological tissue. The threshold that leads from animal to man is crossed when the Holy Spirit unites with the pure force which, tempered by the density of the elements, was developed in nature and became the basic substance for the spirit.

"Man evolved from animal not only physically, but also with regard to soul elements. The Holy Spirit, implanted into the first humans whose mode of life was still animal, caused the genesis of the human race. Mankind was bound to the law of the soul's reincarnation—a necessity of natural evolution. All life grows and matures and so your soul also grew and matured.

"In the great cultural epochs of history, the people, who had become knowledgeable through the extra-sensory perceptions of individuals, entered into relations with the spirit world. They became aware of the demons and gods whom they were able to understand to a lesser or greater degree, according to their stage of development. But the permanent shadow of their form of life was that they were not redeemed. Even the highest spiritual maturity did not accord them salvation and although they received messages from the star-gods, they still remained bound to the law of reincarnation.

"The noblest souls were granted admission by the star-gods to a spheric realm which the Greeks called Elysium, but from there they had no possibility of rising up to God until, due to my own incarnation on earth, the cosmic laws changed.

"Only as man did God open the way of salvation to all souls. A way that leads into the world of supreme happiness. This world, in a myriad magnifications, branches out all over the cosmos on stars of light and warmth, of joy of life and of spiritual fulfilment of tasks. The stars of great maturity, inhabited by men in soul form, are governed by angels of the highest rank; divine beings who are also called princes of heaven. Permeated by the spirit of God, who reveals himself in his angels, these are the realms of the greatest happiness.

"The process of regeneration, which takes place in accordance with the rhythm of eternity, prevents fatigue, monotony and weariness. It is a process which re-charges the vitality of people who are grouped together through racial ties and offers them variations in the tasks they have to fulfil, a change of relationships and domiciles, as well as travels and experiences which are out of the ordinary.

"Heaven is a sublime kingdom spread over many stars. Some of them—by earthly standards—are infinitely remote from one another, but they are connected by paths of energy. These course through the cosmos like veins, so that all the desired stars can be reached by both men and angels as well as other high-ranking spirit beings. Heaven extends around your earth and your planetary system across the Milky Way.

"A look at the stars forces you to recognise your own insignificance in relation to existing dimensions and distances. However, because of the radiations from the Holy Spirit, you have been chosen to colonise the spirit spheres of the cosmos. You are awaited in the realms of light. *You were born to live eternally!*

"Strong currents rise up from the darkness into the light. Man's horizon will expand and penetrate living areas which, until now, were unknown to him. The wealth of life is spread out across infinite star worlds in endless variety. You have been chosen for great spirit tasks on stars you are to colonise, freed from time, which keeps you prisoners here.

"Scientific research into matter explains how sound waves travel. Your thoughts travel in a similar manner. They are received as ray transmissions and measured for quality; then tested, classified and recorded or erased again. The insignificant vibrations of everyday thoughts formed around unimportant matters are not recorded in the book of purity. They dissolve. The standard of value for the maturity or immaturity of a soul is its degree of radiance in a gradation of colours.

"Affiliation to a community of belief alone does not mean an increase in the soul's value. The life force of those who do not obtain the necessary standard of purity cannot be sustained for eternity. Small blemishes—like stains on a white cloth—are redeemable, but if the fabric is damaged beyond repair, no cleaning will help.

"Eternal man must give evidence of angelic characteristics, for only then can he live in the realm of angels, to thrive, grow, further develop his mind and other faculties and show that he is worthy of his Creator. Only when he reaches the demarcations of the necessary soul value, only then is he a human being in the noble sense of the word.

"The relentless laws of nature prove that only the strong and the healthy can exist. In the life beyond, only the pure and the noble can exist. These laws of nature know no mercy. God's sublime will demands everlasting life; he demands it within the framework of cosmic needs. The rich fields of the stars need to be cultivated by spirit beings who can fulfil all tasks through the power and the strength of their souls as much as through the kindness and the tenderness of their feelings.

"This you must know: angels are light-born beings. They are sublime powers of spirit and love. Within the cosmic plan of creation it was necessary that God assign to the light-born, noble, divine beings strong shadow-born souls, beings of strength and purity.

"Therefore, you are not born to be happy, but happily to fulfil great tasks; happily united by the great bond of love which stretches far across the spheres of life.

"Eternal life needs refreshing through manifold changes. This is heaven: love and security, work and success, effort and relaxation, toil and recreation, seriousness and gaiety. You are to live independently integrated into the laws of the divine state, guided by angels and sublime spirit princes.

"You yourselves form the spheric environment. The laws of harmony determine the building of cities and the design of the countryside. Immortal man in the world beyond is permeated by the feeling of God and can therefore not produce anything ugly, so the buildings of the celestial realms are marvels of architectural beauty.

"The artists rejoice in giving heart-felt thanks to the Creator in multiple harmony—in pictures and colour, in shape and form and in the strains of divine music.

"Historical epochs of the earth are maintained in the realms of heaven for the eternal recognition of the spiritual development of mankind. You find ancient cultures preserved in buildings, manners and customs. These are the most splendid museums of creation, living images of the past, which you can visit. They are testimonies of God's power and of the achievements of his sublime will in the struggle for the immortal soul of spirit-imbued man. Time and eternity are counter-graded and distributed among the stars of light. Every person who is mature enough for immortality when he leaves the earth is guided by strict laws to the place where he can continue his development towards the final goal of perfection of mind and soul.

"The soul's path to salvation therefore begins in the zones of purification and continues in the regions of the joy of living. Men feel at home in the heavenly spheres—in the countrysides, cities, villages and meadows, the forests, lakes, rivers and the ocean.

"The eyes of those who have come from the earth are familiar with the flowery pastures, the gardens and fields, the many species of the animal world. All these animals come from the earth. They are integrated into the community of man for his pleasure. Exempt from the earthly law of blood, which demands death in order to preserve life, they now find themselves in the realms of paradise, nourished by the inexhaustible wealth of flora. This world appears to the newcomer to be one of terrestrial naturalness, but wonderfully bathed in the splendour of heaven.

"Man's way of life here is according to the laws of divine order of state. Nobody is left to his own arbitrariness. Bound to the loving heart of his guardian angel, who already guided him on earth, the individual lives here together with his family in personal freedom and dignity, for the purpose of increasing the value of his soul by his own efforts. People are schooled in public institutes of learning so that the unequal state of spirit development of those coming from the earth can be adjusted. Hidden talents are discovered and perfected, secret desires fulfilled and wishes realised, so that divine gifts inherent in the spirit of man are actively developed. In the course of the evolution of this rich and colourful life, radiations of happiness are received through the experience of love and friendship in the rapturous accord of souls in harmony. But the supreme happiness of the heart thrives in the union with God.

In heaven there are places to worship God. These are temples or cathedrals, large, magnificent buildings where people congregate for holy celebrations of love.These celebrations of love and thanksgiving are conducted by priests and priestesses—people of the greatest maturity. They are solemnised as ceremonies of humble worship of the Father, the Son and the Holy Spirit. The presence of the Lord manifests in image and figure.

"I, Jesus Christ, am the Lord of mankind.

"My image, as the living projection of my personality, appears simultaneously in all churches, cathedrals and temples so that my presence, which on earth you can only sense, is visible. In this projection my soul is distributed a thousandfold. This is the miracle of the omnipresence of God. God is both person and radiation. God became man in his son and Jesus the man became God again beside the Father who, beholding everything, stands above all life. So your Lord in heaven as on earth is God and man at the same time—divine projection in human form.

"The radiation of love is in need of response, for the elemental power of this current, which permeates the entire cosmos as the pulse-beat of life, intensifies as it flows back into God's heart.

THE STAR OF SUPREME PURITY

"IN THE universe there is a wonderful star, which we call the star of purity. An infinite number of gifts from God have rendered it more prominent than other stars. Its holy sphere is of the utmost beauty ever to have emanated from the soul of God. The holy beings who inhabit it are chosen ones who through the great purity of their souls have risen above the shadows of the period of maturation to the highest level of human soul value. The path to it is taken by all souls exempt from the spheres of purification and maturation.

"On this star a degree of happiness is attained that cannot be described in earthly words; a happiness that comes from the proximity of the Godhead. Firmly established within the laws of order and governed by innumerable angels, this kingdom of perfection stands in beauty in the sunlight of the Holy Spirit, above the spheric worlds of infinity.

"Holy rivers flow through the country. In meadows similar to those on earth blossom the most divine miracles of nature. God has created mountains and lakes, forests and grass lands for his earth-born darlings. The snow-covered peaks of remote glaciers delight the eye of the beholder; the ocean's waves wash onto sun-drenched shores and the sky pours its blue over the scene. At night, the stars shine in magnificent splendour and proclaim the message of God's eternal presence.

ENCOUNTERS BETWEEN MAN AND GOD

"THERE are many encounters between man and God. The fond Father feels the human heart's need for proof of his divine love, his strength and his power. He gives token of his presence to loving, praying souls through gifts of answered prayers and fulfilled wishes and through dispensations of fate of an unexpectedly happy nature.

"Nobody who beams his heart to God in the most devout love remains unheard or unheeded. But he who cannot give himself to God in humility and love can spare his prayers. Only in the holy flow of love do the prayers reach the highest power of love and achieve miracles.

"From every faithful heart a current flows to God. From the heart of unbelievers this current flows into nothing. A surge and flow streams from your souls into the world of stars and is measured for its degree of radiation.

"Love is a radiation of immense power. The purest, deepest love which diffuses itself in humility to God can bring about a change in the worst of fates.

"And if you love God, then you love Jesus and the Holy Spirit, for the Trinity of the highest love is one. If you enrich your earthly life with this exalted sentiment, you are truly the children of God and nothing threatens you any more on this earth. The happy state of not being dominated by matters of every-day life gives you grandeur and dignity. It gives a regal status to even the lowliest and most modest human being.

"An hour of happy union with God means more to you than all earthly pleasures. You contemplate the affluence of the rich without envy, and pity those of them who are far from God.

"Across the borders of countries you are a big family united in love—a big family united in the feeling of belonging together.

"To search for God means to find God, for no call to the Father goes unheard. Contact with God is also made through conscious perception of the angel, who is the radiation of God, as well as through recognition of the personal presence of God, the almighty Creator of the universe.

"These are the experiences of mystics and people who can lose themselves in God with a feeling of total submission and self-surrender. When all prayers end and culminate in the sole feeling: 'I am yours and only yours for eternity,' then the supreme happiness of life is experienced and God in his glorious appearance is immediately present to lovingly embrace the awakened human soul. God is not bound to his heavenly kingdom; he visits his earthly children and can be present at any moment in any place when the radiance of a soul summons him."

THE HOLY TRINITY

"THE Trinity is very difficult for you to understand. The Lord in the universe of stars is God. His kingdom is the entire cosmos. Therefore, God is the supreme spirit in the universe of stars.

"Think of the Holy Spirit as a current that flows through all eternity and infinity; as a light whose sun-like rays burst out of a supra-cosmic force. The cosmos is confined but, at the same time, infinite, because of its growth. It is a figure of unimaginable size and it is bathed in the light of the Holy Spirit of God which permeates it. The Holy Spirit has the effect of a supra-cosmic sun which also shines on other universes in infinite space, for our magnificent cosmos is not the only one in existence.

"The universe is full of miracles that cannot be understood by the human brain. The Cosmic Spirit, however, is silhouetted against this sun of his activity as a divine figure of unimaginable splendour.

"Through a division of this primal form of God, our Father—the Creator of all life—came into being. It was a division which took place in every spirit atom and resulted in the second form. God, therefore, *is* the Holy Spirit. And yet the Holy Spirit acts as an independent Divinity. He is beyond the cosmos, which is permeated by his rays. The Holy Spirit fulfils tasks different to those of God the Father; tasks which I cannot make understandable to you. The Son came forth from the Father through the power of the spirit. For the love of the people on earth he entered a newborn child whose life was begotten in the body of the pure virgin by the Holy Spirit, the primal form of God.

"Therefore, my people, you must now understand how the Godhead is the everlasting primal power of one spirit and yet lives and acts in three figures."

THE DIVINE ORIGIN OF LIFE

"A DIVINE law of God is the aspiration of the male and female sex to unite. The fulfilment of this law preserves all life.

"Unisexuality is the holy origin of all life. This is God, is God's primal spirit and it brought forth God and the Son. This is how the Trinity came into being. It brought forth sexless, angelic spirit beings, but it did not bring forth a mankind with an immortal soul. Therein lies our Father's great, miraculous power: that he divided the original concept of unity, thereby preparing the eternal flow of procreation. The God of creation aspired to a mankind that basically never separates and yet develops separately.

"In the angels' sparkling existence the enchantment of the union of individuals is also experienced. God the Creator, who permeates all life, is the spirit of love. Through his power of love the holy, undulating rhythm of attraction came into being, to give birth eternally to new life and keep old life young.

"Our cosmos only preserves its shape through the immense binding power of love; this cosmos which, constantly growing, resembles a giant whose scaffolding of stars is like a human skeleton, whose undulating current is like human blood, but whose soul gains durability only through the immortal souls' incorporation into the entire holy organism.

"The embryo is a simile for development. The primal thought, the perfect human being, is in every female ovum, in every male sperm and grows after union. The perfect human being resembles God in appearance, but the way to perfection is long. The perfect human being in the world beyond has angelic beauty and an angelic nature.

"In every act of procreation God's sublime mission is imprinted into the human embryo in the holy moment of union of the ovum and sperm—the mission to strive for the soul's perfection. In the embryo of the earthly body is the complete human being with his genetic code.

"The human mind develops already in the embryo. The implantation of the astral body takes place at the moment of the child's separation from the mother's body. When the umbilical cord is cut, it has already been implanted. It spreads throughout the physical organism and integrates fully with it. The brain of the soul takes on the mental impressions and imprints of the physical brain."

MY ORIGIN

"I POINT out to you that in human form I was the son of God. Through the materialisation of the divine generation in the body of the blessed virgin, the ovum was fertilised. Materialisations are not unknown to you. So you can understand that the supreme God of the cosmos could bring about his son's human existence through the materialisation of his divine semen."

MY EARTHLY DEATH

"THOSE who crucified me and wanted my ignominious death were severely punished by God; for it was not God's will that I should die in such a way. His will was to test the people and to test the power of my love.

"If I had not been crucified, but had been recognised by the people as the son of God, the picture of mankind would have changed. A happy race would have prospered, bathed in the light of salutary stars. But the people stood weakened in the shadow of ignorance and demanded my life. And heaven demanded my sacrifice.

"I was to live—or to die—for mankind. The happiness of man, which I longed for, was not to be achieved in the earthly sphere. However, after my resurrection it flourished in a wonderful way in heaven for the mature, noble and devout souls. The last direction I gave was the confirmation of faith through my appearance after death.

"When I lived as a human being, I believed that by the power of my spirit I would be able to lead my people and afterwards the other people of the earth, towards a glorious future. But I was advised that my Father, who beheld the hearts of men, desired from me that I fulfil the most difficult task that could be demanded of a young, proud mind—to suffer humiliations meted out by base, vile souls in the sublime consciousness of my own greatness.

"To be degraded, spat on, ridiculed and tortured unto the death of the physical body; to give away the blood of the Father flowing in my veins; this was enjoined on me. I suffered it a first time at the Mount of Olives in Gethsemane in the darkest hours of my life, but I anticipated it in a thousand pre-sentiments.

"Oh you humans, I know the pains of the soul as much as the pains of the body! The son of man was human, with all the fears, all the pain. Many have suffered after me and triumphed in death over the evil in the world, as I triumphed over the spirit of evil whose traces have survived only in man, only on the shadowed earth. For the infinite cosmos thrives and prospers in the omnipotence of God. Many have suffered after me, but no one has suffered the pains of man and God at the same time.

"I sacrificed my heart for you, so that you might rise up to God's world. Now once again I am here on earth, so that the new age can begin. It will guide mankind one step higher towards the light; nearer to the Father than ever before.

CONDITION

"I ENTER all *human souls who surrender themselves to God and purify them. My love enters them, but so does my severity. My grace and indulgence fills a soul dedicated to God, but so does my reprimand. This means: God is a spirit of* condition. *No man lives without the conditions of God, nobody can escape them.*

"If a soul shines for God on earth, fulfilling his conditions and doing justice to his standards, then I pour the radiation of my being into this soul. These radiations in individual human souls are markings. They shine in the over-shadowed circle of the earth and illuminate it.

"The light reflected by these blessed souls is guided by God, in accordance with a cosmic condition, into the spheres of the Holy Spirit. In this way the light of my soul is dispersed all around the world like glittering crystals, some of which sparkle like beryls, others like diamonds; like precious stones that have received the power of light from the pressure of the earth's forces.

CONSOLATION

"EVERYONE should bear his life's burden with humility, for in this way God assesses the strength of a heart.

"No one who gives his heart to the eternal heart of love, who presents his soul to the soul of eternal God, remains without being strengthened, without being comforted.

"No one travels through the dark stretches of his fate without light. The fountains of love flow for all of you.

"Kneel down in humble resignation and accept the burden of this life on earth! And if you stumble and fall under the cross of sorrows that burden you—like God's son on his most onerous walk—then call on my angels of love that they may strengthen you.

"For even God's son broke down under the burden of the suffering of this world and he was strengthened by the power of love, so that he could give himself completely for you.

"The wounds of this world all heal in my pain and in the days to come all life will flourish and prosper in happiness *in the love of my heart.*

"With reassurance every soul may await life in the kingdom of eternity, in the kingdom of sublimity and may nestle into the arms of the Father, in joy and in sorrow.

"Angels are God's tenderness, feel it in every hour of exhaustion!

Messages from Mary

JESUS
(received at the forest crucifix on 11th June, 1982)

"JESUS is of such majesty and dignity, of such sublimity and grandeur as no human mind on earth can divine.

"Miracle upon miracle reveals itself to you when you enter the world of the blessed, but the greatest miracle of all that awaits you is Jesus.

"His love is as vast as eternity.

"His love penetrates the innermost depths of those who are exiled and expelled and compels the salvation of countless souls from whom God's mercy would have been withheld, in accordance with the iron rules of the cosmos.

"Jesus works with the tireless commitment of his heart, his energy, his radiations and the angels who serve him.

"His figure is that of a tall and perfectly handsome man. His countenance is divine harmony, with an expression of heavenly sublimity:

Ecce homo—ecce Deus!

"No one who lives in our world and is called by him, to kneel before him and receive the tender touch of his hand upon his forehead—does so without tears."

MANKIND TODAY
(received in the church of Maria Wörth, 27th August, 1982)

"IT IS the wish of Jesus that you make known how involved his soul is with the anguish on this earth. Make known that the shadows of human corruption and depravity reach up into the spheres of light; that hope battled with despair in his heart before he decided to save mankind from destruction; that he spreads his hands over the pure souls on this earth to check fire and death.

"Infinitely many seeds of human souls still lie in the garden of expectation and shall come to bloom on this earth.

"Without the concentrated power of his will, the sons of God in the stars would stand powerless and paralysed by pain, confronted with the grief of the Father. Powerless and paralysed by pain, they would let mankind perish in the chaos of its own making; this mankind which deems itself great and knowledgeable, strong and powerful, but which is more miserable in life and administers the wonderful possession of this planet more contemptibly than any human race before."

WARNING
(received at the forest crucifix on 2nd May, 1982)

"IF YOU do not begin to feel shame and repent of the critical lack of your love, a star-power will be aroused; an eternal power that knows no mercy.

"If purification and change are not effected, if greed for power finds no bounds, if your hearts remain cold and cannot be kindled by the fiery rays of God's love, then the spirit of horror will take possession of this earth.

"The Godhead is resolved to exact this last trial from mankind —without forbearance, without the leniency of the very highest judges.

"If the love of Jesus for mankind should perish here in the dust of base minds, the Godhead is determined to let an important and divine eternal law take effect; a primal law of the nature of the cosmos; a law which demands destruction where depravity is rampant.

"For before one organ of the body begins to rot and damages the entire organism, it is destroyed.

"Oh you people, do not withdraw from the holy course of events which the Lord allows to occur in order to rescue you!

"Without Jesus the world is lost, without him there is no salvation and no future for mankind!"

PRAY TO JESUS
(received at the forest crucifix on 12th August, 1982)

"DIVINE power is at work throughout the worlds, divine thoughts order the cosmos. But Jesus, despite his unimagineable tasks, is always tranquil, sublime and free. His spirit and his soul are *always* free.

"In the halo of his glory the forces, powers and hosts of angels are at work. Like a sun he towers above them and yet he has human form, human nature and human feelings.

"Therefore, always turn to him without reserve—even in the confusion of earthly life and its daily involvements. Turn to him, for he will never consider a prayer to be a disturbance."

Various Statements

OSARIO ABOUT JUPITER

"WE CALL the ruler of the planet Jupiter, Emilius. His radiation influences all mankind. If he is favourably positioned in the constellation at birth, he brings luck and success to a human life. If you have the firm will to live happily and successfully, you can increase his influence. Every human being has the opportunity to be happy, even if his stars are not initially favourable. The secret of happiness and good fortune is a strong will and the firm conviction that it can be obtained.

"It is possible for all of you to turn to the star-gods and ask them for help, or to attract their attention by powerful thoughts. They are the executors of the very highest will. Therefore, never forget to turn to God in love and gratitude at the beginning and end of your prayer.

"God is a spirit whose greatness and importance you cannot imagine. He is the most sublime spirit in the universe, and his will permeates the entire cosmos. The love of his heart shines upon all life and flows through all life.

"The fortune and misfortune of man does not lie solely in the stars, but in his heart. It is a secret that I would like to reveal to you: your happiness is the great goal of God. You are meant to be a free, happy and blessed human race, but you must know that true happiness is often different from what you imagine it to be. It is not wealth, which can even mean misfortune; it can cause considerable harm to those who have it; it can impoverish their souls. True happiness includes a knowledge of the sorrow of life.

"Everything fulfils itself in a happy human life. A soul must be able to bear bravely even the difficult hours of earthly life, in order to mature for true happiness—to which you must all aspire. Emilius strengthens your hearts and paves the way to happiness."

SIXTUS ABOUT PROSPERITY AND OBLIGATIONS

"Life on earth is only a prelude to
the symphony of real life."

"NOBODY should strive to achieve superficial happiness, for it betokens trouble. Those who live constant care-free and light-hearted lives will be assigned difficult tasks after their deaths; they will have special obligations imposed on them and special achievements demanded of them in order to make up for their idle existence on earth.

"If they lived nobly, that is to say they were good and decent people, then they have the possibility of achieving a higher soul-ranking and an increase in spiritual value by fulfilling tasks in the dark areas of the spheres. If, in their earthly lives, they were dominated by human weaknesses such as excesses of pleasure, vanity, pride, unkindness to their fellow men, brutality to those weaker, coldness and mercilessness to animals, indifference to the pain and suffering of others, hypocrisy, falseness, garrulousness ("vile gossip" as you call it), they will have to languish for a very, very long time in the zones of purification before they can reach higher light zones. But if, in spite of these weaknesses, they remained good people, then—after their enjoyable life on earth during which they luxuriated in prosperity—they are delegated difficult tasks.

"So the gods adjust the fates of men. For those who have to bear sorrow here may this be a great comfort, because this sorrow is only a first step towards the greatest happiness in future life. You cannot imagine what a great leveler heaven is."

SIXTUS ABOUT PRAYER

"The Lord is present in his
angel, both vocally and silently."

"ALL people shall listen more intently to the inner voice, shall bind God's angel to them through prayer. In this way very much suffering will be avoided, or mitigated and reduced. Every human life on earth is improved by the angels' guidance of the individual.

"Teach your children to pray. The parents' daily prayer forms protective currents over the children. All parents should invoke the angels of their children and talk to them. Through God's supreme grace and love they will then remain close to you.

"People pray far too little. The prayers of love that reach God are much too weak. Send strong currents up to heaven! Call upon the Father from the depth of your hearts and give him your love every day in good, clear words."

SIXTUS ABOUT DISEASE AND HEALING

"THE soul participates in the healing process of every illness. I refer to the astral body which is controlled by emotion and feelings. Those feelings, which express themselves in thoughts, cause currents to flow into the stricken tissue. If the feelings are negative, as is the case with obsessions, fears, dejection and resignation, the currents are also negative. The strong, beneficial cosmic currents are denied entry.

"There are many damaging currents on earth. You all know how the weather affects your health. You can be harmed if you live over a water course; you can be affected by radio-active rays. The moon and the sun, as well as more distant planets, influence you. Even the earth damages your health through currents from metal and radiation fields which form on its surface. So your life is continuously threatened and you are in danger of losing it.

"But you can arm yourselves against this threat with holy currents from the cosmos. A widespread field of energies lies above you. From it the angels draw their strength. When you are out of luck and helpless, when illness and sorrow weigh you down, remember this and ask God for help. Through prayer the angels are granted the ability to channel the power and the wealth in the atmosphere directly to you and your physical body will then be able to overcome the threat. All of you are protected by your angels, otherwise you would perish.

"You who read this have gained knowledge. Attract the currents of heaven more strongly and even the most hopeless illness can be cured."

SIXTUS ABOUT HIS WORK

"IT IS my divine mission to intervene in difficult fates—a mission I fulfil in the spiritual radiation of God the Father, the almighty ruler of heaven and earth, of time and eternity, of space and infinity, of light and shade.

"I cause the holy star of hope to shine where vital power is needed. I attract all the energies that give courage and stability. I delight the sacred host of guardian angels by inspiring open-minded people, as well as purifying the hearts and minds of insufficiently enlightened, doubting and searching doctors whom I aid in their work of healing.

"It is not possible for the light of heaven to penetrate totally into the realm of gravity. The cosmic powers are bound to nature's earth currents.

"The loving angels strive with all their might to preserve earthly life. They shield the people entrusted to them with their protective rays and strengthen their will to live.

"Most people do not have sufficient psychic power to await their death with resignation—the inevitable death of the body. Only unusually strong souls are able to do this.

"Every purification process in the body pre-supposes the will to live. When the dark currents in the blood of man disappear, new happiness of life on earth is granted. But only for a certain time. No wanderer on this star can escape the sublime laws of the powers of fate. Only the time limit until the end of life on earth can be extended. Sometimes considerably.

"Here you are only the *seeds* of *life,* meant to come into full bloom in our world—seeds, which we lovingly care for and protect on this dark earth.

BENEDICTA—ABOUT THE LIFE OF ANGELS ON EARTH

"WE ANGELS are vibrations of light in the radiant aureole of God. We angels are souls who have always remained in eternal light, sprung from the love of God. Only the gloom of this earth over-shadows us. We only feel deep grief for the suffering of this earth. If God were not to strengthen us, we would perish in this earth's stream of suffering. If we did not receive the radiations of his force, we would be weary unto death in this sphere of affliction.

"You loving souls are our only happiness here; your mute, fervent words of love our only joy, your thoughts our only light.

"Thoughts hallowed in prayer, sprung from the innermost depth of the human heart are the source of love granted to us here. Here, where we too, yes we too, have to stand the test of the eternal, rigid law which says:

"You shall lighten the darkness. You shall warm those who are cold, sweeten those who are bitter, pardon those who have failed, relieve those who are burdened, bring joy to those who have knowledge!

"This earth is dull and dreary, cold and dark for us angels if your hearts do not glow for us here, if your souls do not reflect the light of God. We live without joy on this hard star, without joy among the people of this earth, if you do not beam to us that which God has implanted in you: the spark of light of his eternal glory which is within you, the reflection of his human soul which is revealed in Jesus.

"Nevertheless, we are happy to be among you if this is granted to us: if your souls expand—permeated, consecrated and hallowed by the immeasurable love of the son of God. Only so do you belong to us. Only so in this most sublime vibration."

Questions and Answers

JESUS ANSWERS MY QUESTIONS

"IN THE Gospel according to John it says: 'I came forth from the Father and am come into the world. I leave the world again and go to the Father.' Does this mean that you were God's son and were incarnated, or did you only come to be God's son here on earth?"

"I am descended from the star-realm of the Holy Spirit, but I became God's son of man only through this life on earth."

I asked about the eucharist, for as I had not been brought up in the Christian faith, I did not understand it. Jesus wrote:

"When my disciples were together with me for the last time, the general sense of what I told them was: See this bread, it is my flesh; see this wine, it is my blood. It is my blood that you take into you when you drink this wine. It is my flesh that you take into you when you eat this bread, for it is the desire of my love to enter into you.

"It is the prayer of my soul that this food and this drink, handed to you, may give you the happy feeling of unity with me. Even as this bread and this wine are taken in by your bodies, so shall my soul be taken in by you, so that my soul's fire may flow through you like this wine and my love strengthen and satisfy you like this bread."

Once, while receiving a message, I was impressed by the beauty of the language and, thinking of Jesus as a man of his time, the question came to my mind:

"How do you come to speak such good German?"

My hand was guided very gently, as if accompanied by a forgiving smile and I received the answer:

"Who, do you think, developed the languages of civilisations?"

MARY ANSWERS MY QUESTIONS

"YOU think of all the tears I shed for Jesus? Yes, my daughter, it was terrible what happened at that time. But I knew that Jesus would live on and that he was the son of God. This helped me to bear this hardest of sufferings. I worried about Jesus throughout his life. As a reward for the many years of fear, I was blessed to see the son of God resurrected. I saw him in wonderful transfiguration."

"Did he look different, better than before?"

"Oh, even as a human being Jesus was a very handsome man; that is to say, God gave the incarnated man a wonderful face. In his transfigured appearance Jesus has actually changed very little. He looks quite magnificent."

"You sometimes show yourself to particularly receptive people, as you did at Lourdes. Why do you appear in this manner?"

"It is because I love people and give them as much help as I possibly can."

"You see such a terrible amount of suffering; how can you live with it? Are you happy?"

"Oh my heart, happy? We live in bliss in our world. And we look upon all the suffering of this earth as one looks upon small, temporary illnesses."

"But some people have to endure such awful fates here. Knowing this, how can you be happy?"

"Man lives on earth to prepare himself for the real life. These earthly pains pass away. Yes, I know what it means to suffer, but it only lasts a short time compared to the eternity of the blessed life."

"And what about the misery of innocent animals which are tortured and abused here?"

"Their suffering also passes. And their little souls are matured and finally raised. But this may be too difficult for you to understand.

"Oh my daughter, we live in a wonderful, celestial world. There is no more suffering here for people or animals. Even if you were to live a thousand years on earth, you could not imagine the supreme joys God confers upon immortal souls."

SIXTUS AND BENEDICTA COMMENT ON MY THOUGHTS ABOUT THE CRUELTIES OF THE INQUISITION

SIXTUS: "All those who committed atrocities in the name of God have been sentenced; they have been horribly punished according to the laws of justice. But do not let those mentally degenerate, insane devil-hunters, who disregarded the religion of love and mercy in a shocking way by torturing and burning at the stake, be your yard-stick for passing judgment upon the Church.

"Think of the great, noble builders and keepers of pure Christianity, who were always God's joy. Do not think about events whose explanation lies in the bloodstream of a primordial, demonic heritage. It is the sublime goal of the holy love of God's son, Jesus Christ, to overcome this, absolutely and finally."

Benedicta: "Put aside those oppressive thoughts and give your Creator your soul's joy of life. All the terrible events that have occurred dissolve in the face of the bliss of eternal life; vanish in the vibration of the heavenly joy of existence like a bad dream vanishes in the reality of a bright, sunny morning.

"Horrible caricatures of man emerged from the soul-scum that formed above a great number of noble souls. Souls, like wine, must mature. Fermentation makes young wine foam, but finally the desired transformation of the grape—the wine—gleams glowingly in pure crystal, and nobody remembers the foam."

BENEDICTA

(In a dejected mood I had been thinking about the deplorable state of affairs on earth; about human wickedness and baseness and about the suffering of the innocent.)

Benedicta commented: "Be happy and cleanse your thoughts from the filth of this world.

"Bear in mind that the noblest, loveliest and most marvellous thought always take precedence over all that is earthly!

God forces the evil in man to destroy itself. The self-destruction of evil is what you call "hell". Every atrocity, every evil deed of man reverts to him."

"Can God not prevent evil?"

"God's power is absolute, but it is his will that man develops independently."

"But haven't we angels to help us. . ."

"Yes, if you call upon them, if you allow them to guide you. If they can stay close to you, then they strengthen you."

"When can they not stay close to us?"

"When your heart and mind are blocked to divine radiation."

"And if this is an illness? A mental illness, for instance, because somebody received too little love, or had to experience too many disappointments, or because he is hereditarily handicapped?"

"If a person is hereditarily handicapped, it means that the body is disturbed. A disturbed body can damage the soul, just as a disturbed soul can damage the body. If the soul is damaged, the angel withdraws, in accordance with a cosmic law."

"But that is very sad, because this is just when man needs his angel!"

"The angel withdraws and observes the person in his charge. Every thought is examined, every feeling considered; every deed and every reaction judged."

"When you angels withdraw in such a manner and only observe and examine, do then other, evil powers act and influence man?"

"Yes, evil powers are very soon present when a person lets himself drift, but they are completely powerless when he calls upon his angel."

"But what if a person is too ignorant to call upon his angel; if he is unbelieving, if he is a child or an adolescent and therefore immature?"

"Then other powers intervene; the most exalted judges and observers of soul development. They evaluate the essence of life and adjust the fate accordingly. This means they lead the person to other groups of people; to other relationships, so that his inner nature can develop in a better way. People are guided to each other for the purpose of mutual growth."

ANGEL'S REPROACH

BENEDICTA: "You are irritated by the painful recognition of your weakness. Your behaviour is being evaluated and judged! Therefore, set aside temper and irritation and learn to control your thoughts—those which are too closely tied to earthly matters.

"You have suffered and see no sense in it. You weigh yourself down with thoughts of anger, reproach and self-accusation. But in every life there are unforeseen injuries, upsets and losses. Therefore, do not complain! Man is often prey to difficulties, but the bond of love with the supreme heart diverts many reverses.

"In such cases God does not want repentance and self-accusation. What God wants is the mastery of earthly grievances, pains and mistakes which everybody can make. To face what has happened and to steer the rocking boat unerringly forward—towards the holy shore!

"If you suffer a small misfortune, it occurs so that you can stand the test. If you pass it, heaven in turn will allocate you a small happiness which was not included in the blue-print of your fate. Rewards for successfully passing tests relating to upsets and losses, annoyances and troubles are seldom given as late as in heaven. On the other hand, sorrow and suffering earn greater gifts of love than such small gifts of fortune.

"Succeeding means achieving self-control without drawn-out complaints and accusations, without remorseful self-recriminations, without pointless feelings of resentment and fury against the one who caused the loss. Clear recognition of the mistake committed is sufficient and serves as a warning for similar situations in life.

"But after the realisation man should attain the tranquil insight of reason, accept the inevitable and remember that all earthly experiences are only a step by step ascent, during which everyone may stumble and fall once in a while."

BENEDICTA ANSWERS ADDITIONAL QUESTIONS

"IS IT true that all angels were once human beings, as Swedenborg says?"

"Angels were not human beings, apart from those who volunteered to incarnate. The evolution of mankind can be read in the book of life by millenia, but angels are souls of God, and God is eternal.

"The holy secrets of human incarnation have never been entirely revealed, not even to the initiated and enlightened of this earth. The soul of man is God's greatest miracle of life. Infinitely varied, it is a creation of light and shade, infinitely inspired by awakening to the glorious recognition of God and infinitely blessed by the Creator's command of love.

"The human soul which has attained supreme spiritual maturity is angelic—therefore, purest, divine vibration."

"Was Mary the incarnation of an angel or of a goddess: for instance, of the star-goddess Hera, or Gaya, or Rhea or Kybele?"

"Mary sprang from the earth as the purest flower, hallowed by the soul maturity she achieved. The divine had to unite with the human, so that the son could be born as God and as man. Mary therefore stands above the thrones and the powers; she cannot be compared with either the known or the unknown most sublime female angelic beings. She lives without equal in a rank of regal divinity."

"Were Gaya and Rhea goddesses?"

"They were not goddesses, but human conceptions of a primal, feminine, child-bearing deity. But the primal power of God does not only give birth; it begets and gives birth at the same time. It is the will of the Holy Spirit to bring forth life.

"Do not attempt to understand fully God and the Trinity. You will learn this in the higher spheres, but I want to add that the word: Father for God is to be maintained. Jesus is the independent Son in the unified will and feeling of God. Jesus is a man in the supreme spiritualised sense.

"The male and female sexes are equally apportioned in the spheres of God. The love relationships of the star-powers and the angelic beings greatly exceed human concepts of marriage and sexual union. They are necessary impulses of life, necessary too for mankind on earth."

"Is God both male and female?"

"God is above the concept of male and female. He is the supreme power of love which surpasses everything existing in time and eternity. His feeling is radiation to every soul and from every soul. His sublimity and power of mind are incomprehensible for you as human beings, but his love can be felt by you in happiness.

"God's love is universal union, universal marriage; it is tenderness in the holiest sense. Nestle close to God like children and you will feel it. Angels are male or female in the most sublime perfection."

Again to Swedenborg: "Why did he write that there was no Trinity of three persons, but only one God and he was Jesus?"

"Because Swedenborg's visions were also limited. The Trinity of three persons was contrary to his basic mental and emotional outlook. The intimations of heaven have to be in harmony with the basic vibrations of the soul of the receiver, otherwise imprecisions occur.

"Moreover, Swedenborg's explanation is not wrong in so far as God lived in Jesus. Every sentiment of Jesus radiated into God's soul. The Saviour also healed the wounds of the Father's heart through the power of his love. The human mind, which has evolved through experiences, can barely grasp the father-son relationship of God. It is not comparable to a human father-son relationship.

"The Holy Spirit is the radiation of God, all-observing universal being and a force that spans all life."

"Jesus spoke to me of "dark powers" that can lead us into temptation. What did he mean? Are there devils or demons?"

"God's holy spirit radiates through the cosmos. This current represents love of life and joy. It does not flow through the shadow world of punishment. The shadow zones are necessary for the purification of souls. Those who execute the penalty are robot-like creatures without heart or feeling, used by the angels of the shadow world. Without a trace of emotion they carry out whatever has been assigned to an individual once he has been condemned. For instance, whoever tortured or murdered here must himself endure the full sensation of the pain he inflicted.

"No sublime spirit being, therefore no angel or highly evolved human being would be able to re-enact such disgusting deeds as are committed by godless people. These robots or phantoms are what men have often perceived and have considered to be devils. Their appearance is ugly and they have terrifying faces, for they are dead creatures, merely mobile tools which are switched on and off for the execution of punishment.

"The dark powers which can influence you are human souls whose baseness keeps them bound to the earth. They seek to fraternise with equally inferior souls who are susceptible to evil, whereby they hope to increase their power. They are not always "poor souls" patiently and repentantly hoping for redemption; they are often very evil souls who know quite well that they have to return to the shadow world where they have already been. They hate all that is noble and pure, against which they are powerless and attempt to influence people whose thoughts hover on the brink of evil. They seek to win them over and lead them into temptation.

"In accordance with the law of free development of mind and soul, which corresponds to the law of nature whereby only the strong multiply and the weak perish, they may exercise their influence for a certain time until—summoned back to the so-called "hell"—they take the long road through pain and night to the distant light of a reincarnation.

"Pray to God that he may keep them away from you when you feel weak and pray to Jesus that he may shield you from every evil influence. These "devils" are depraved human souls.

"Demons are earth spirits. They come and go. God does not pay attention to them. They are waste products of soul elements and they disintegrate in the same way as they form. They do not exist in highly civilised cultures. They have their origin in the wild, primordial urges of primitive people; in some tribes of indigenous races they still exist today. Through missionary services, which must be prudently and tactfully practised, they will disappear there too."

"Are there also good human spirits working here? And does it occur that former relatives, members of the family, or friends are allowed to visit the earth?"

"Yes, there are highly developed human souls who work on earth, just like the angels. They come from the spheres of light and strengthen you. And members of the family or friends are allowed to help their dear ones on earth if they have a strong desire to work here. But for this they need special permission, which must be granted by an archangel. The majority of the blessed live on wonderful stars in the world beyond."

"Did the so-called fall of the angels take place?"

"There was such an event during a star epoch of cosmic evolution. It was like a severe cosmic disease which can never return."

"Was Lucifer the prince of the world mentioned by Jesus in John 16/11?"

"He was, but his obstinacy was crushed. His initially exalted nature bowed in shame before the power of love evinced by Jesus. Lucifer is not to be placed on the same footing with the conception of the medieval Satan with horns and claws. He is really a prince with star-god status. His stellar companion is the ruler of Saturn, that power which introduces hardship into your lives in order that your souls may mature and strengthen. Souls who have to endure for eternity cannot be permitted any inherent weaknesses."

"Lucifer has to abide by the will of God. No man need fear him, if he binds himself to God and Jesus, or if, instinctively, because of the natural purity of his soul, although he is unreligious, he listens to the divine voice of his conscience and observes it in his way of life. Pray to Jesus! Even the over-powering blows of fate from Saturn are mitigated and some-times prevented by the protection of the love which Jesus grants to all who trust him.

"Lucifer rules the shadow world as an organising spirit. His nature is scintillating and inscrutable. He is a picture of splendour, but lacks the warm radiation of divine love. The light of his torch will be extinguished as soon as God lives in every heart on earth. Then the shadow world will disappear like a small ulcer on an otherwise perfectly healthy body. Then God will assign other tasks to Lucifer and the angels who serve him."

"Does Lucifer live in what we call hell?"

"No, he lives on a star of light. The other dark angels, too, have a zone of happiness in which they are free from all the pulsations of the transient suffering they behold. In the days to come, Lucifer and all the dark angels will be changed and granted the divine grace of oblivion."

"Hildegard of Bingen writes that she saw the devil tied up in hell. What did she see?"

"What she saw were stirring images of the spheres beyond that were both happy and distressing, but she was not able to interpret everything she saw correctly. Her mind, like the mind of every human being, had a limited receptive capacity. The great secrets of the divine world of stars will be revealed to you only after millenia of spiritual growth and evolution.

"People who believe in a strong Satan see God as a weak spirit, powerless before the evil one and they try to assist God by struggling against the devil. However, God's Trinity is absolute omnipotence."

Here Sixtus took my hand and wrote:

"You, my child, think too much about dubious legends. Lucifer broke the pledge of obedience. God assigned him the task of separating the bad human souls from the good ones, and punishing them. Through punishment the bad souls are fundamentally changed, so that their basic soul substance can be transmitted—either back to earth or, in individual cases and guided by loving souls, upwards into the brighter zones of purification.

"Many legends have sprung up around the Fall. But even the highly evolved spirits and mature human souls in the spheres of light, who sometimes communicate through mediums, lack clear insight into this cosmic event and do not have exact knowledge about the spirit of resistance which Jesus conquered. They give you interpretations of the possibilities, but no clear insight into the reality of a by-gone epoch of the history of the stars. God's cosmic events are an ever-lasting secret for the blessed.

"Lucifer defies explanation. His name means "carrier of light" and his light tests human souls without mercy. His life is a sealed mystery.

"The basis of the construction of the universe is aspiration and resistance. Purified of resistance, God's stars now wheel in their courses. The world of stars is populated with celestial life and everywhere order prevails. Obedience to God is the principal law of the spheres, whose harmonious tone sounds through the universe."

Benedicta: "Pray to God the almighty, and nestle close to Jesus with profound love. The Holy Spirit radiates upon you whenever you pray. I give you a:

Prayer to Jesus Christ

Jesus Christ, you my God and Lord,
are great as eternity.
There is no power above you
except the power of your spirit
which brought you forth.
You became the Saviour of mankind.
The God of the cosmos consecrated your life
to the divine goal of his creation:
a noble and sublime human race.
As man in God you stand
above us all.
You spread your love across the earth
as God's sun does its rays.
Before the radiance of your heart evil vanishes
as veils of mist in the light of the morning sun.
The jubilation from a billion hearts,
that rises up to you,
will wash from this earth
all that abhors the union with God.
Happiness on earth will grow from the seed
you sow in hearts of steadfast faith.
Conscious of a blissful future,
mankind will rise
from the nadir of the present
and admit your spirit.

                                        Amen

Angels to their Charges

SEMIDIAN TO AN EIGHTEEN-YEAR-OLD

"YOUR attitude has now matured sufficiently for you to understand how much God desires the love of man. God needs this love, so that he can beam it back on to those of you who live here without thinking of the Father in heaven, the Creator to whom you owe your lives. His love shows you the path you have to tread on this earth. Now, consciously and with your angel, go this way.

"Listen to me, my child. I dwell close to you. Where you live, but in another sphere, I have a home. So we angels live with you. I always hear you when you speak to me. Call to me and I will be close to you; then tell me your wishes and the favours you want granted, at the same time showing me your pure heart. I can do very, very much for you if you ask for it.

"The flow of prayer that emanates from your mind gives me the power to direct particular holy currents back to you, in other words, to help you. Without your prayer I would not be able to intervene.

"So always remember that you have a soul close to you who loves you very, very dearly and tenderly. Give me the purity of your soul, the love of your heart and you will master this life on earth as God intended you to. I know you intimately. Never be ashamed, before me, because of the natural feelings which God has implanted in all you humans. We angels only evaluate the soul. Keep it pure, my child! Everywhere I am with you, but grant me the joy of your prayers to God."

DANIELA ON SELF-REALISATION

"YOU do not know which path to follow? Your angel has to abide by the laws of God. Life is self-realisation, which means you mature through your independence, even if you make wrong decisions.

"Therefore, none of your paths is wrong. You will find shadow and light everywhere; everywhere they will be allocated to you.

"Do not be afraid of incorrect decisions; do not weaken yourself through worries. Go briskly and cheerfully towards your future. Rise above the irritations of every-day life. Be happy and show God that you have spirit and energy, for in the days to come you are to rise up into the world of strong and mature souls.

"If you feel weak and over-burdened, call upon Ervinius. Deiamos gives you all the favourable radiations from his star, Mercury. Be certain, you have the help of heaven, but you must act and decide for yourself."

BEATA TO AN EIGHTY-YEAR-OLD

"MY beloved, deeply troubled heart, I want to give you a present, so that you may understand the reality of my existence.

"You think you are old and believe your life is coming to an end. You consider the days that may still give you the joy of life as days of grace. When you add them to your years of life, look back, but forget time, for time is nothing. Be happy in the knowledge that your inner self was not formed by your past years, but by the wealth of those moments when, from eternity, the reflected glory of supreme feeling and perception shone down on you.

"Love, friendship and music as well as the joy of a mother's heart have been granted you in abundance and have always been the great pleasure of your soul. And so it will always be. Do not count the years that have passed, nor seek to calculate the years that may still remain to you. Be certain, there is no end! If you doubt this, then like a stubborn, inexperienced child you are mistaken. Your future is as great, as rich and as vast as it was at the beginning of your days on earth.

"You ponder sadly that "Nothing is harder than a parting", just as if a farewell was very near. But what is in store for you, is an increased joy of life; a joy of life that you can only appreciate in your heart when you think of love and youth and beauty and happiness—and all of them enriched by one word—'infinity'.

"Just as your soul has remained young within the robe of your body, so it will endure. Be happy and live! Strengthen yourself in the course of your days by directing to God your thoughts, which you should put into words of prayer. Do not be afraid, be happy, my heart."

CONSOLATION ON THE DEATH OF BELOVED ONES

DIANIDA: "The future in God's world is as real as life here. Parting causes hearts sorrow. But how wonderful it is to know that the land to which the beloved one had to travel is of indescribable beauty. Death is an illusion. Death is nothing!

"Do you shed tears when you lay aside a worn-out garment? Why tears? Life is glorious and eternal. Be happy about it! The angel speaks holy truth."

LISARA: "I have flowers from the gardens of heaven for you. Even if you cannot see them, I will still decorate your home with them. The death you are mourning does not exist. Your mother has risen into a beautiful world. She fell asleep and awoke in the presence of an angel, who received her. Matured and pure as a blossom, her soul entered a sphere of light where she was awaited and received with great joy.

"The end of her life was full of grace. Pain and suffering were spared her. The angels arranged that you be removed from her at this hour, because she needed rest, which your anxious heart would only have disturbed.

"Your mother always gave you love, help in life, strength and support. So now give her soul peace by submitting in humility to the divine will of God.

"Do not weaken your life force by painful yearning. Nestle tenderly close to your angel, who transmits your thoughts to your beloved mother as if they were letters.

"Many tasks remain for you to fulfil on earth. Strengthen yourself through prayer and feel my presence every hour, my grieving, brave heart."

SEMIRA ABOUT THE CONVERSION TO FAITH

"YOU, my most beloved heart! Happily I dwell close to you every hour, for you have given me roses from the garden of conversion. Your roses continue to bloom in my heart.

"You have returned to the Father. You have nestled against the heart of his son. The fountain of your hot tears, which broke forth from the depth of your soul, flows towards great, holy streams—the streams of love to God. You have overcome shyness and doubt. You have become aware of divine feelings and full of repentance you now realise your aimless wandering through life's past years. You look back in shame and know of God's love, which you failed to recognise before.

"Look up now to the stars! Raise your eyes to heaven!

"Your heart can achieve *everything*. Life's burden and pain are nothing. God watches over you every hour and accompanies you through his angel. The blood's holy bond with the heart of the Lord of eternity will enrich and strengthen you.

"Jesus needs you and your devotion; he needs your rich gift of prayers. Do not be shy. Request and receive everything which his immeasurably wealthy heart has allotted to you.

"So, as if you were standing alone before him in cosmic space, love him and receive his love!"

WORDS FROM JESUS

HOW obviously Jesus Christ is present, and how much he honours the missionary zeal of individuals is shown by his message to a friend of the Usebius Circle.

"I greet you, my beloved son! Your return to the Father is blessed! Your deeply felt devotion to the Lord of mankind, Jesus Christ, points you to the way of salvation. You have put aside all doubts. You grant me glowing streams of divine love. From the heart vibrations of the people you lead to me, you build a temple of humble sublimity in which your affiliation to me finds its consecration. Your love is a deep well from which your Lord, bowing down, draws water to still his heart's thirst.

"Your Lord is blood and flesh and soul in eternal life; he is ardent desire and he is solitude if the holy waters of love from such wells are not offered to him. You will open many more of these wells for me. I now count you among my disciples—the disciples of today. In flowering gardens you and your life's companion will one day receive the gratitude of your Lord and from the abundance of roses you will bind me bouquets.

"I want to hand you the cup of wisdom, so that you may drink from it to honour the Godhead who, even on earth, sprinkles you with the dew of his grace."

Jesus Christ

Epilogue

EPILOGUE
May 1983

SIX years have passed since the world beyond broke into my life; since that first wonderful encounter with the angel who conveyed to me God's message that I was to write a book. And still, day after day, I experience the miracle of the divine reality, which was disclosed to me then.

I am sometimes asked if I have constant contact with my angel. Yes, I understand my Benedicta when she speaks to me and I always feel her closeness, but she does not answer all the questions that people put to me. Everyone who asks will receive help from his own guardian angel and can learn to understand him through feeling and perception.

Like most women I am busy with the duties of a home and a family, and I find some hours of privacy for prayer and meditation.

Benedicta orders me to lead a quiet life.

"Confine yourself to your divine task! A combination of solitude and the company of dear friends is appropriate to your vocation and important in your life."

Talks with my friends, but most of all the total understanding of my husband, which I now have, helps me to bear the often difficult, and sometimes overwhelming, impact of this wonderful experience.

The present condition of our planet is serious and sad, and two messages I received from Mary pose a heavy counter to the words of joy, which I received from Jesus at Easter, 1982.

On 1st February, 1983 Benedicta gave me the following words in the little pilgrimage church at Birkenstein:

"Mary is exhausted by the suffering and pain she has experienced for mankind. She will withdraw her protective mantle of love if no purification and maturation of human souls occurs on earth. Very strong radiations of love are needed to refresh the heavenly mother again. Holy rays of love from human hearts."

Let us remember the message from Mary: "Mankind Today" received on 27th August, 1982 about "this mankind which deems itself great and knowledgeable, strong and powerful, but which is more miserable in life and administers the wonderful possession of this planet more contemptibly than any human race before."

If we do not change, we will again experience a "quiver of God's soul" which, like the plague in the Middle Ages, will carry off people in their thousands before "the page of history turns" as Jesus has prophesied. We have been warned—the forests are already dying.

But hope is given to us by Benedicta's words of 1st March of this year: "Marvels will occur, for the threat, which is world-wide, will open the hearts of men! Jesus is penetrating the hearts of thousands. His tidings of salvation are imparted, in brilliant words, in all radiations, in all colours, in all languages, in all mental as well as spiritual gradations. Warning signs are being placed. And you are one of them.

"The nature of man is manifold and can only be reached in different ways. Many people need harsh words to tauten their souls; others, like children, require detailed advice. Some seek the way to God through evidence of psychic existence, in other words, through experiments with the supernatural. Others search for God in asceticism and deep prayer, in meditation or self-conquest, through abstinence, renunciation or purifying penance.

"Others are healed from serious illnesses and see in this the love of God. Still others feel God's presence through divine surges of great music and the nobility of language . . . So many mediators are necessary to awaken all souls.

"Your pure and sublime offering of divine words to mankind shall be dedicated to those who are mature and strong in soul and rich in the heart's power of love. In our world they will fulfil noble deeds for God and will serve in the great work of creation in the cosmos.

"Mankind will recover, as an afflicted man recovers from bouts of fever and newly risen from the severe illness, will cause God to rejoice."

During a recent stay in Kärnten I received new messages from Mary, which I offer in conclusion of this book.

The Mantle of my Love

"The mantle of my love grants you protection. I shelter you in it from all evil.

"The mantle of my love is wide, and it envelops you all who pray and are but children calling for their mother.

"And all of you are my children! I am the feminine sentiment of eternal God, I am his tenderness and grace.

"Through me, as through a holy diadem, he shines down on you, and the radiance of his soul touches you more softly in the mirror of my heart.

"I am the bond that unites the human and the divine.

"I was the purest chalice of humility to receive God's glory.

"And I bore the son of light who, with the power of love as man and God, transformed the cosmic laws, and made the world of salvation available to you.

To the Discontented who complain about their Life's Adversities

"Thousandfold, laments of life rise upwards—the bitter laments of life. Do you expect life's full, exalted happiness already on earth? Are you not content to know that you are God's children? Are you not content to inherit what the Father has built up for you over billions of earth years? Are you not content to grow into eternity, which he, the star worlds' supreme spirit has prepared for you in a thousand heavens of bliss? Are you not content to know: I am, I live, and my heart beats through him, for him, consecrated by the supreme son's prayer of love!

"Do you not recognise yourselves, do you not see yourselves in your unworthiness?

"You live and complain—complain, but live!

"You gaze into the sky stretched blue above you, receive the sun's gleaming light in the warmth of the verdant earth, behold the stars of your universe wheel in their orderly paths, receive love's gifts over and again—gifts in time and eternity . . .

"Oh, you people, does it not suffice to be the most blessed souls of immortality? Do you want to drink dry the golden chalice of happiness already here?

"Fill, oh fill your ungrateful shadowed hearts with the radiance of God, with the radiance of the angel's soul, the angel who dwells close to you! Master your errant feelings and rise out of the poverty of your self-centered thinking, out of the confines of your fear of existence. Throw aside the daily complaints and irritability, and show it to God, so that you may be counted, weighed and not be deemed too light in the measure of the highest judges.

"Rise to pure love, you people, to pure love, which is also prepared to bear the burden laid upon you by fate's mysterious designs.

"Be humble, as Jesus was when he carried the cross, be proud in the most noble meaning of the word, for he was too in the knowledge of the glory of his soul.

"And all of you, too, know of your souls' divine origin!

"Be happy! For you are never alone. There is a divine feeling around you, a wonderful consolation and understanding, a gentle, tender caress and comfort.

"And all, all is understood by the angels, all that is human.

"Nestle in God's arms when you are sad, and the angel of his mercy shelters you, embraces you and envelops you in his heart's radiance, and strengthens you from the holy stream of God's eternal love!

This my beloved daughter, I give you as a solace for the world.

Mary

Some Examples of
Handwriting

Jesus Christ

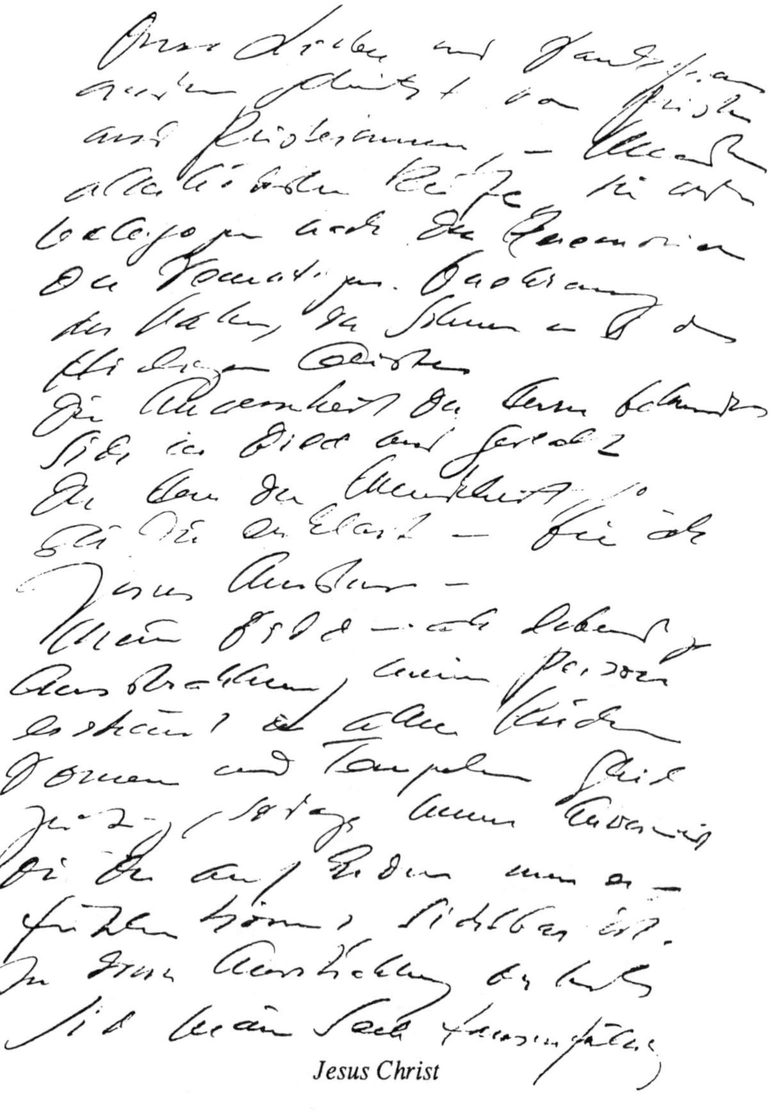

Jesus Christ

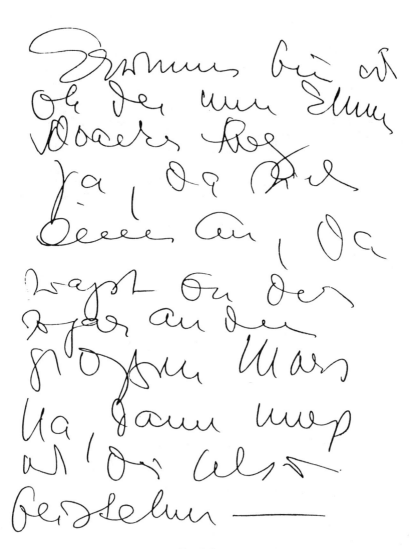

Erwinius

Above: Sixtus
Below: Gerda Johst's handwriting

Hearing

Julie Haydon

Contents

Hearing

We hear with our ears.

Hearing is one
of our five senses.

Sounds

This boy can hear sounds.

Sounds are all around him.

He hears lots of sounds

in a day.

Some sounds he likes.

Some sounds
he does not like.

5

In the Morning

It is morning.

The boy can hear a sound from his clock.

It is time to get up.

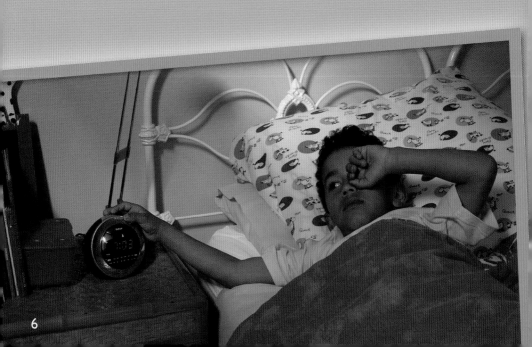

The boy talks with his mother.

He can hear

his mother's words.

Walking to School

The boy and his mother walk to school.

They can hear cars on the road.

They can hear a train.

It is not safe

to walk over the **tracks**.

At School

The boy can hear

the school bell.

He can hear his teacher, too.

Now the boy can hear music.

He likes the music.

He moves to the music.

Lunchtime

The boy plays with a ball at lunchtime.

He can hear the ball hit the ground.

He can hear his friend
calling to him.

At Home

The boy goes home
after school.
He can hear his dog barking.

The boy plays with his dog.
They make lots of sounds.

Glossary

tracks